THE BUSINESS-GOVERNMENT RELATIONSHIP
A Reassessment

Edited by Neil H. Jacoby

Foreword by Harold M. Williams

Proceedings of a Seminar at the Graduate School of Management
The University of California, Los Angeles

Sponsored by the Norton Simon, Inc. Foundation
Commission on the Business-Government Relationship

January 24–25, 1974

GOODYEAR PUBLISHING COMPANY
PACIFIC PALISADES, CALIFORNIA

Library of Congress Cataloging in Publication Data

Main entry under title:

The Business-government relationship.

  Bibliography: p.
  Includes index.
  1. Industry and state—United States—Congresses.
2. Industry—Social aspects—United States—
Congresses. I. Jacoby, Neil Herman
II. California. University. University at Los
Angeles, Graduate School of Management.   III. Norton
Simon, Inc. Foundation Commission on the Business-
Government Relationship.
HD3616.U46B87   338.973   75-15547
ISBN 0-87620-129-X

Y-129X-4

Current printing (last digit):
10 9 8 7 6 5 4 3 2 1

Printed in the United States of America

Contents

PART III   THE DIALOGUE

PART IV   THE PRODUCT

Foreword

Effective collaboration between government and business is a central requirement for dealing with most of the major problems facing American society today. Many of today's unresolved issues are a consequence of the failure of business and government, the two primary institutions in this society, to function effectively, individually and in relation to each other. Disappointment over this malfunctioning has led, increasingly, to the disenchantment of the American people with both institutions.

The desire to improve this condition led the Norton Simon, Inc. Foundation for Education, with the encouragement of its Board of Directors, to establish the Norton Simon, Inc. Foundation Commission on the Business-Government Relationship, with initial funding of $1 million. The importance of the task prompted Dr. Roger Heyns, President of the American Council on Education; William W. Scranton, Chairman of the Northeastern National Bank and former Governor of Pennsylvania; and Sol. M. Linowitz, Partner of Coudert Brothers, former Chairman of Xerox Corporation, and former Ambassador to the Organization of American States, to join me as members of the Commission.

The timing of the grant was influenced by two factors: First, the growing importance of the issues; and second, a desire to recognize the retirement of Norton Simon from active participation in the company he founded by the establishment of a substantive activity of consequence to society in a field in which he has had a deep commitment and a continuing interest.

The selection of the Graduate School of Management at UCLA as the basic site for the program was logical. I am Dean of the School, as well as chairman of the Commission and former Chairman of the Board of Norton Simon, Inc. More importantly, this School has over the years devoted much of its talent and resources to business-society relationships. Indeed, the School has been a leader in research and teaching many aspects of the interaction between academia, business, and government.

For example, in recent years the Research Program in Competition and Business Policy, led by Professor J. Fred Weston, has been engaged in important, original, empirical work resulting in basic revisions in the theories of the role and impact of large firms on the U.S. economy. The Center for Research and Dialogue on Business and Society, led by Professors George A. Steiner and Neil H. Jacoby, both scholars of international reputation in this area, has contributed valuable publications, teaching materials, and conferences. It has encouraged dialogues among businessmen and academicians to enhance mutual understanding and promote progress toward better business-government relations. The School also has provided leadership in international and comparative management, multinational corporations, and business and government planning in an international framework. Faculty members in organization and management theory, quantitative methods, behavioral sciences, sociotechnical systems, accounting, and marketing have also made substantial contributions to knowledge about public-private sector interactions.

The Commission in its early deliberations became convinced that the formulation of principles to govern business-government relationships was a task of utmost importance, and one that should not be confined to the conventional themes of government regulation of business, subsidies, or procurement policies. The sense of the Commission is that the United States has entered an era of intense international competition for world resources and markets, and that our progress as a nation—perhaps even our survival as a world power—will depend heavily upon the effective and productive interaction of the public and private sectors. These changing conditions will have a profound impact on such matters of vital concern as individual freedom and centralization of government. As a result, the Commission concluded that the inquiry into the business-government relationship must be couched in the broadest possible context and must have a positive thrust.

As the Commission's first effort to explore this very broad field, a small group of distinguished and intellectually innovative individuals was invited to discuss proposed priorities at the Graduate School of Management, UCLA, in January 1974. Each participant was requested to prepare a paper, to be distributed prior to the seminar, setting forth those aspects of the business-government relationship the improvement of which he considered to have the greatest potential payoff for society. At the seminar the papers were discussed and priorities established. Although this seminar was not called to produce a publication, the quality of the papers was so high and the discussion so provocative that the Commission decided to publish these proceedings.

The Commission wishes to express its deep respect and appreciation to all participants in the seminar; to Professors Jacoby, Steiner, and Weston, of the Graduate School of Management at UCLA, who served as advisors in the establishment of the concept and substance of the seminar; but particularly to Professor Jacoby, who served as seminar chairman. With the assistance of Professor Kovach, he also edited the transcript of the proceedings into the accurate, coherent, and well-articulated text presented here.

Harold M. Williams

Dean, Graduate School of Management, UCLA

Acknowledgments

I am grateful to the many persons whose efforts made this book possible:

First, to the authors of the papers and the participants in the dialogue, who graciously consented to my editorial surgery on their material.

Second, to Assistant Professor Carol Kovach, who completed the herculean task of making sense out of the transcribed tapings of the dialogue. Without her preparatory work, any coherent editing would not have been possible. (We now fully appreciate the obstacles confronted by Chairman Rodino of the House Judiciary Committee in deciphering the Watergate tapes!)

Third, to Mrs. Grace Marshall, who gave the final product a very competent editing for style and format.

Fourth, to Mrs. Lynn Hickman, my secretary, who conscientiously supervised the typing of the edited manuscript.

Above all, of course, I thank the members of the Norton Simon, Inc. Commission on the Business-Government Relationship. Their vision, personal interest, and financial support constituted the foundation on which the seminar and this book were built.

Neil H. Jacoby
Graduate School of Management, UCLA

Part I

THE PROBLEM

CHAPTER 1

The Symptoms of Malfunctioning

Today, nearly everyone agrees that the business-government relationship in the United States is in trouble. A faulty interaction between these two most important institutions of our society has resulted in a piling up of unresolved social problems. Effective cooperation between government and business is a sine qua non of sustained social progress; the fact that during recent years the forward momentum of our society has faltered—and occasionally stalled—suggests an unsatisfactory interface between the public and private sectors. Add to this a disturbing lack of confidence by the American people in both business and government, and it becomes clear that improvement of the relationship between them—and thereby in the performance of both—is a matter of primary importance, and even of urgency.

AN EXAMPLE: THE ENERGY CRISIS

The energy problem vividly illustrates the malaise we are discussing. During the autumn and winter of 1973–74, the cartel of oil-exporting countries quadrupled the price of crude oil, and the Arab members cut back production and placed a temporary embargo on shipments to the United States. The ensuing energy crisis revealed an appalling lack of preparedness to deal with this emergency by both the U.S. government and the U.S. petroleum companies. The federal government had no contingency plan ready to put into effect, although the nation was importing 30 percent of the oil it consumed, and the catastrophic effect of an Arab oil embargo could easily be foreseen. Even an adequate base of information was lacking. There was no accurate measure of stocks of crude oil and petroleum products in storage, in the pipelines, and in transit on the oceans.

Most appalling, however, was the general ignorance of the respective responsibilities and roles of the federal government and of the oil industry. Public officials blamed oil executives for failing to anticipate the embargo. Many even charged that the heating oil and gasoline shortages were contrived to swell petroleum profits! Petroleum executives castigated public officials for delaying the issuance of antipollution rules and permits, which would have enabled them to site and design refineries and electric power plants. Senators Frank Church and Henry Jackson headed Senate committees of inquiry into energy shortages in an attempt to find scapegoats. Emotional proposals were made to nationalize the petroleum industry, or to subject it to public utility regulation—sure roads to industrial paralysis! Instead of rational, cooperative action by the public and private sectors—each doing its respective job—there was a spate of name-calling and scapegoat-seeking, and a lack of effective remedial action.

The 1973–74 energy crises showed once again that American society is crisis-actuated. It temporizes and debates while problems expand into crises. Then, more often than not, it overreacts with hasty programs of action not based upon adequate study. The basic need today, therefore, is a firm and well-conceived federal energy policy. Such a policy would embody rigorous energy conservation measures to reduce crude oil imports in the short run. It would set ambitious but realistic targets for the expansion of domestic energy supplies in the long run. It would reconcile environmental improvement with energy needs. And it would provide profit incentives to the energy industry to expand domestic supplies.

The role of government as a political institution is to weigh the goals and values of society, to fix priorities and trade-off relationships, to lay down the rules, and to motivate private enterprise. The role of business as an economic institution is to act vigorously, within the parameters set by government, to satisfy the demands of the public as expressed in the marketplace. There is a lamentable want of understanding and acceptance of these basic truths today.

REASONS FOR IMPROVING THE RELATIONSHIP

There are compelling reasons why improvement of the business-government relationship now warrants a prior claim on the attention of scholars, businessmen, and public officials. The postwar economic renaissance of Japan and Western Europe has created intense international competition for world resources and markets. The ability of the United States to compete effectively in this new multipolar world depends upon an effective interaction between government and business. Concerned Americans are asking whether the traditional relationship—widely described as "adversary"—is optimal for the future.

This issue has been sharpened by the burgeoning of multinational corporate enterprise throughout the world, with American-based companies playing a leading role. Multinational business has, of late, encountered increasing hostility at home and abroad. American trade unions would put a tight checkrein on the operations of multinational businesses by sponsoring such legislation as the Burke-Hartke Bill. Other critics propose to monitor and control multinational business through new international agencies. The U.S. government has maintained an attitude of neutrality toward the foreign operations of its corporations in recent years. The problem of defining an optimal business-government relationship thus has a foreign as well as a domestic dimension.

The contemporary cry for "social responsibility" also has revealed much misunderstanding of the nature of the business-government relationship. Many fail to distinguish the social responsibilities of government from those of business. Although business can be properly criticized for its insensitivity and unresponsiveness to changes in social values (e.g., auto safety and emission control), it should not be castigated for failing to correct conditions that require prior action by government. Air and water pollution is an example. It is the unique responsibility of government to fix the standards of environmental quality desired by society. A business that incurs heavy expense to clean up its operations—in the name of "social responsibility"—suffers grave disadvantages in comparison with its competitors who do not do so. Only government can make and enforce laws that are binding upon all firms, and which leave their competitive relationships undisturbed. Businesses are incompetent to weigh social values: indeed, it would be arrogant of them to do so.

All of these considerations lead to the conclusion that efforts to make the U.S. business-government relationship more productive will have a very high yield. A better relationship will ameliorate many social conditions that trouble us today.

THE DIMENSIONS OF THE RELATIONSHIP

So far we have spoken of the business-government relationship, but it is apparent that this collective noun embraces a multitude of interactions. Merely to list them all is not easy. If we view these relationships from the perspective of *governments*—federal, state, and local—we can see that governments relate to business enterprises in at least the following ways:

—They attempt to *stabilize the economic environment* of business through fiscal, monetary, and "income" policies.
—They *subsidize* some types of businesses, as those engaged in farming and shipbuilding.
—They *promote* American business abroad through trade fairs, information services, favorable taxation as applies to the DISCs, etc.
—They *finance* small and minority firms and housing enterprises through direct loans and loan guarantees and insurance.

—They *purchase* military hardware, construction, and many other commodities and services from private enterprises.

—They *enter into joint or mixed ventures* with business, as in the cases of COMSAT and OPIC.

—They *tax* business, and they *make business a tax collector* for government in the cases of alcohol, tobacco, gasoline, and other excise and sales taxes.

—They *regulate particular functions of all businesses,* such as competition, foreign trade, political activity, labor relations, issuance and sale of securities, safety of products, financing terms, and environmental emissions and impacts.

—They *engage in joint management* of "public utilities," regulating entry, territory, output, investment, prices (rates), and other variables of operation.

—They *sell* postal services, nuclear fuel, electricity, government publications, police and fire protection, and many other commodities and services.

The foregoing interactions constitute the *economic* dimension of the business-government relationship, because they all pertain to business products, costs, prices, and markets. And all of them flow from government *to business.* Although it is clear that governmental action dominates and generally establishes the environment within which business functions, there is also a counterflow of business economic influence *upon government.* Thus the capital-expenditure policies and production plans of business firms help to determine the level of output, employment, and income of the nation. The products and services designed by businesses, and the trade practices they follow, influence the legislation passed by Congress and the rules of governmental regulatory agencies. And the pricing policies of business may either retard or accelerate the inflation that has afflicted the nation in recent years.

But there is also a *political* dimension to the relationship. Like the economic dimension, it includes business activities intended to influence government as well as governmental actions to constrain business. The types of business political activities that bear upon government include:

—*Consulting* by businessmen with government officials, either informally and individually, or formally and collectively, through such organizations as the Business Advisory Council and the Committee for Economic Development.

—*Supporting candidates* for public office—financially and in other ways—by business executives and business organizations.

Politically-oriented actions of government that affect business include the regulation of lobbying, restrictions on contributions to political campaigns, and constraints on the employment of former military officers by defense industries.

In the political as well as the economic spheres, the business-government relationship is clearly one of action, reaction, and interaction. Many government actions support and promote the private sector, while others burden and restrict it. This is equally true of business influences on government; some are supportive and constructive, while others are negative and disruptive. Looking at the whole set of complex interactions between the public and the private sectors, observers differ sharply on whether—in the aggregate—the influence of government or business predominates, or whether an optimal balance of power prevails. Some critics hold that government is "in the pocket" of big business, and they describe the United States as a "corporate state." Other observers see the private sector so heavily burdened and restrained, and so bereft of economic and political power, that it is losing its dynamism at home and abroad. Many contrast the "adversary" relationship between business and government in the United States with what they believe to be a "cooperative" relationship in Western Europe and Japan.

THE UCLA SEMINAR ON THE RELATIONSHIP

No doubt it was the complexity, the importance, and the malfunctioning of the American business-government relationship that led industrialist Norton Simon to establish the Norton Simon Inc. Foundation for Education, to conduct a major ongoing program of study on this subject. The Commission's first public undertaking was to sponsor a two-day seminar at UCLA on January 24 and 25, 1974, to explore the field and to identify needs and priorities. In addition to the members of the Commission, the participants included four business leaders, four heads of institutions concerned with public policy research, and seven university professors in the social sciences. Each of these participants will be introduced in Part II of this book, wherein their papers are presented.

The seminar combined prepared papers and dialogue. Each participant was invited to write a ten to fifteen page paper, describing those issues within the business-government relationship that he considered to be of the greatest concern. Papers were submitted by fourteen participants, and these were all circulated in advance. While differing markedly in their approaches, perspectives, and assignment of priorities, there were discernible points of consensus, which will be discussed in Chapter 8.

The participants' papers were analyzed at UCLA, and the agenda of the seminar was based upon this analysis. The agenda called for three sessions of dialogue devoted, respectively, to diagnosis of the current business-government relationship, assignment of priorities to particular topics for research and education, and a strategy for implementing a program of research and education. A list of leading questions was drawn up and grouped into these three categories. The aim was to strike a felicitous balance between freewheeling and structured dialogue. All discussion was tape-recorded and transcribed.

THE ISSUES DISCUSSED AT THE SEMINAR

The following issues were posed for discussion:

Diagnosis of the Problem

1. How should the present U.S. business-government relationship be characterized?
2. How does the U.S. public view the relationship
   a) now?
   b) prior to World War II?
3. Has the relationship been improving or worsening?
4. Why is the relationship not as productive as it could and should be?
5. What changes in American society have affected the relationship
   a) in the social structure?
   b) in social values?
6. What changes in the external world and in the U.S. role therein have affected the relationship?
7. What are the salient causes of a less-than-optimal relationship?
8. How does government prevent a good relationship
   a) by its structure?
   b) by its administrative processes?
   c) by its policies?
9. How does business prevent a good relationship
   a) by its structure (e.g., concentration)?
   b) by its economic actions?
   c) by its political activities?
10. Is the present boundary between the private and public sectors
    a) indefinite?
    b) improper (i.e., inefficient)?
11. Is the political power of business conducive to an optimal relationship?
12. Is communication between business and government adequate?
13. Is the relationship in the United States as productive as that in other large countries?
14. What features, if any, of the relationship in other nations should the United States emulate?

Topical Priorities

1. What are the main *gaps in knowledge* of the existing relationship
   a) in the United States?
   b) in other countries?
2. What are the key *areas of public ignorance* or misunderstanding of the U.S. relationship?
3. What *priorities* should be assigned to the following topics
   a) Promoting business-government collaboration in resolving social problems
   b) Drawing boundaries between the public and private sectors
   c) "Reprivatizing" some governmental programs
   d) Public financing of election campaigns
   e) Reforming governmental regulation of business
   f) Regulating by means of market forces versus government commissions
   g) Educating leadership in roles of government and business
   h) Legitimating government's economic role
   i) Legitimating business' economic role
   j) Achieving growth-oriented taxation policies
   k) Promoting competition in the U.S. economy
   l) Developing governmental intervention in the U.S. economy
   m) Studying business-government relationships in other leading economies
   n) Reducing conflicts between multinational companies and national governments
   o) Stimulating self-regulation by business
   p) Investigating new types of public-private enterprises
   q) Simplifying state and local governmental structures
   r) Restraining the rise of governmental expenditures
   s) Learning about business-governmental cooperation from the defense establishment
   t) Implementing the planning function in government and business

Strategy of Implementation

1. In a program of action to improve the business-government relationship, what relative emphasis should be placed on
   a) research to discover new knowledge?
   b) synthesis of existing knowledge?
   c) dialogues and conferences?
   d) formal education?
2. What persons are best qualified to staff such a program?
3. What institutions can collaborate most helpfully?
4. What are the necessary and desirable time dimensions of such a program?

5. What are the financial requirements of an effective program?
6. What are the best ways to publicize the program and maximize its influence?
7. What are the next steps the Commission should take?

All these questions can be summed up in four generic inquiries: What is the current status of the U.S. business-government relationship? How does the public perceive the relationship? What should it be? How can it be made more effective?

The papers and the dialogue of the seminar were addressed to these issues.

Part II

THE PAPERS

CHAPTER 2

The Changing
Societal Environment

*Four of the papers written by participants in the seminar were primarily con-
cerned with the contemporary societal environment in which U.S. government
and business interact. These papers diagnose the causes of public dissatisfaction
with both institutions, and probe the causes of malfunctioning in the relationship. They explore the ways in which changing social values and new technological developments create both problems and opportunities for business corporations, and give rise to higher public expectations of their performance. Finally,
they suggest paths along which public and private policies might be directed in
order to create a more productive relationship in the future.*

*Daniel Bell ascribes the altered relationships between business and Ameri-
can society to the emergence of a national and a communal society, to a rising
public belief in "entitlements," and to a deeper concern for the quality of life. A
laggard corporate appreciation of these basic changes led, in his view, to over-
reactive regulation by government, as the case of the U.S. automobile industry
illustrates. A massive shift has occurred in our society from* market *to* political
*decision making, and this has congested our obsolete political system. Professor of
Sociology at Harvard University since 1969, Bell previously served on the faculty of Columbia University, and before that on the editorial board of* Fortune
*magazine. One of the nation's best-known sociologists, he is the author of ten
books and numerous scientific articles.*

*Kenneth E. Boulding focuses on the factors that cause institutions and
ideas to gain or to lose "legitimacy" in the public mind. He points to shifts in the
legitimacy of such concepts as economic inequality, profits, and the work ethic.
And he proposes that an intensive investigation of the dynamics of legitimacy
could be the key to a better understanding of the U.S. business-government relationship. A distinguished economist, Boulding has in recent years worked in the
field of social theory. He has served as Professor of Economics and Director of
the Institute of Behavioral Science at the University of Colorado since 1968.
Educated at Oxford University and the University of Chicago, he previously
served on the faculties of Iowa State, Fisk and McGill Universities, and the
University of Michigan.*

*L. Earle Birdzell describes American government and business as engag-
ing in guerrilla warfare, when both should be collaborating to enhance the pub-*

lic welfare. In his perception, the political influence of business is dangerously weak, both because it espouses an individualist ethic in an increasingly collectivist world, and because, unlike other institutions, it lacks a political constituency. The main hope for a less abrasive business-government relationship in the future lies in the emergence of a better integrated and more mature urban society. A lawyer by profession, educated at the University of Chicago and Harvard University, Birdzell is a member of the corporate executive staff of the General Electric Company. He is a perceptive observer of institutional relationships in U.S. society.

Simon Ramo *argues that technological changes are a central driving force in creating social problems and thus the need for new institutional structures to cope with them. Illustrating his thesis by the examples of developing mass rapid transit, creating new cities, reducing pollution, expanding energy supplies, and dealing with impending revolution in information technology, Ramo concludes that the United States now has a* hybrid economy, *and that it must develop new types of public-private organizations (a "social-industrial complex") to cope with the problems of our times. Vice-chairman of the board of TRW, Inc., Ramo is a scientist and engineer turned industrialist. Educated at California Institute of Technology, he is an expert in microwaves and guided missiles. He was a cofounder of Ramo-Wooldridge Corporation, which merged with Thompson Products in 1958 to become TRW, Inc.*

TOO MUCH, TOO LATE:
REACTIONS TO CHANGING SOCIAL VALUES

Daniel Bell

THE CASE OF THE AUTOMOBILE INDUSTRY

A little more than a decade ago, the automobile manufacturers were mainly unregulated private enterprises. They were free to design the kinds of cars they pleased, subject to consumer acceptance. Their marketing practices were a marvel of precise management and control. Their pricing policies were geared to provide a high rate of return on capital, based on a standard volume concept. Today, auto companies are subject to detailed governmental regulation in which almost all phases of design, marketing, and (at times) even pricing policies are responses to specifications laid down in Washington. The conferences of top auto managements are preoccupied with cost and design problems arising out of the ever-increasing number of government regulations.

In 1960, the automobile had become the shining example of capitalist enterprise. If, in the Soviet Union, the only triangle according to official ideology was boy-girl-tractor, then, in the United States, each man was in love with his auto as well as his wife. The automobile was large, comfortable, and flashy. The freeways were long, fast, and carefully banked. The auto gave each family not only a status symbol but also unparalleled mobility and freedom.

The industry itself had settled down to an extraordinary era of good feeling. The bitter years of labor strife were now behind it. Bargaining could still be tough and the strikes occasionally rancorous; but the industry had learned to live with collective bargaining, and government pressures had largely receded. Moreover, the industry had become conscious of its responsibility to the economy. In 1954, the announcement by General Motors of a $1 billion expansion program was credited with heading off a threatened recession. As Professor Abram Chayes commented: "GM's management might as easily, and perhaps with equal justification, have put the $1 billion in dividends or wage increases or price cuts. Yet the choice, having such profound public effects, was a corporate decision."[1] The one abrasive issue confronting the industry was the charge by various dealers that the companies had practically unrestricted rights to renew or cancel their franchises, and the dealers had no recourse against such arbitrary power. In response, Congress passed the automotive-dealer franchise legislation, which, as Kingman Brewster commented, " . . . comes closest to bearing out the Berle 'due process' prescription for corporate accountability."[2]

There were some clouds on the horizon. One was the nagging problem of auto accidents. In 1950, motor vehicles accounted for 34,000 accidental deaths. By 1965, they accounted for 49,000, and the gradient was rising steeply.[3] Another cloud was the smog spreading from the southern California freeways, blanketing the valleys, and creating hazards for aviation, vegetation, and the human anatomy directly by causing an increase in the incidence of pulmonary diseases. The simple fact was that the auto industry dragged its feet, and then turned away from these problems. In 1956, Ford made a serious effort to sell a safer car; but this was followed by a bad sales experience, and the industry decided, apparently, that a concern for safety was bad for business. On air pollution, some small companies began experimenting with emission controls, particularly after bills providing for air standards were introduced in the California legislature; but the big auto companies either did little or sought delaying actions. Their attitude was that consumer reaction was all that counted, and that consumers did not want to be troubled with safety devices or with emission controls.

It is instructive to review the kinds of constraints under which the industry now finds itself.

Safety.   Because of federal standards, an auto designer now has to take into account: restraints (including seat belts, balloon bags, buzzer systems), specifications for brakes, visibility of fields, inside padding, strength of bumpers, safety glass, bonding of paint, etc.

Noise.   Inasmuch as the auto industry will have to reduce the decibel levels, the designer, particularly of trucks, will have to be concerned with the engine, fan, exhaust, transmission, etc.

Emission of Pollutants.   The air standards require a radical reduction of hydrocarbons, carbon monoxide, and nitrogen oxide.

Fuel Economy.   New legislation seeks to insure that all automobiles will achieve a standard of fifteen or even twenty miles to a gallon of gasoline; this involves horsepower, size and weight, extras, such as air conditioning, etc.

In the halcyon days of laissez faire, the classic doctrine of the market was *caveat emptor.* This was thought to develop the mercantile virtues, making buyers and sellers sharp, cautious, and resourceful—a band of Yankee traders setting the standards of exchange. Beginning about fifty years ago, the legal doctrine began to change; "the minimum of goodness" became a test that commodities had to possess to be marketable, and warranties against defects became a necessary cost of production. In 1959, the extraordinary case of *Comstock* v. *General Motors* disclosed the uncontested facts that the Buick Roadmaster had a defective power-brake system, and General Motors had to issue two separate kits for the replacement of defective parts. Yet, as the Michigan Supreme Court stated in its findings, "No warning to owners of these 1953 Buicks . . . was given either by General Motors or by the agency which sold this Buick as far as this record reveals."[4] Today, each auto company now publicly recalls hundreds of thousands of automobiles if serious defects have to be corrected.

In instance after instance, the automobile industry has been forced to public accountability by legislation or by court action rather than by voluntary initiative. Why did the auto producers go wrong? One thing is clear: The industry failed to understand some significant changes in American society and is now paying the price in the form of detailed regulation. As is so characteristic of U.S. government responses to a whole variety of political and economic issues, (is it a national character or a failure of decision making?), government reaction comes "too late and too much." We temporize, inflate problems into crises, and then react with an overkill.

BASIC CHANGES IN SOCIAL STRUCTURE AND SOCIAL VALUES

The changed relations between business and society derive, in great measure, from two structural and two value changes that have taken place in the United States during recent decades.

1. The National Society. During the last three decades, for the first time in its history, the United States has become a "national society." It has been a "nation" ever since the Articles of Confederation were replaced by the Constitution of the United States. Yet only in the last thirty years, primarily because of the revolutions in transportation and communication, have we become a "national society," in that shocks and impacts felt in one part of the country are immediately reproduced and felt in every other part. Through the revolution in transportation we have cross-country jets that carry a traveler from the Atlantic to the Pacific in five hours. Through the networks of communication we have coast-to-coast telephone dialing in "real time," the simultaneous publication of national newsweeklies in every part of the country and, of course, national radio and television.

One of our difficulties is that we have not learned how to manage a national society. About the turn of the century, we became, for the first time, a "national economy," in that we were able to create national markets because of the railroad. In retrospect, one of the achievements of the New Deal was to work out, through trial and error, the mechanisms for managing a national economy. We often forget how recent are such tools of macroeconomic measurement as concepts of national income or gross national product. National income accounts were first created in the Department of Commerce in 1942, and the idea of gross national product was first proposed in President Roosevelt's budget message of 1944. Few persons would assume that we have mastered the art of economic management, yet few would doubt that we have come a long way from our fumblings in the 1930s.

The problems of the national society are, primarily, the problems of health, education, welfare, and the physical environment. These are summed up in the "quality of life" concept. We have increased the national income substantially, but few would assert that the quality of life has increased proportionately. We do not have a national health policy, or a comprehensive national welfare policy, or a consistent national educational policy. We have made a start toward an environmental policy but, as with so many other developments in American life, our actions have been "too late and too much."

2. *The Communal Society.* We have become, as well, a "communal society." One dimension of this change is the rise in the number and scope of "public goods"—goods and services that are purchased or produced by government for all of the people. Weapons are an obvious example. During the American Revolution each man brought his own musket to the army; it was an individual good. Today, all weapons are purchased by the government. So are a variety of other goods and services that an individual cannot efficiently buy for himself. Government expenditures today account for about 30 percent of GNP—a measure of the enormous relative growth in public goods.

A second dimension of the "communal society" is the extension of "externalities," a word almost unknown to the public a few years ago. Externalities are costs (or occasionally benefits) that are generated by one party (be it corporation, municipality, or private individual) but are borne by other parties or by the whole society. Noxious emissions into the air or disposal of wastes into the water are familiar examples. The important feature of externalities is that, except by resort to the courts, the only way they can be "internalized" and borne by the responsible party is by public authority, which makes rules or levies penalties applicable to all parties that generate such costs. Necessarily, this means the extension of governmental powers.

3. *Entitlements.* Economic growth brought with it, as we know, a "revolution of rising expectations." But a modern society brings with it also the sense that each person is *entitled* to some minimum, decent standard of living: That he has a "right" to a job, to protection against the hazards of unemployment, old age, accident, and illness, to decent housing, and other amenities. In the United States, we have had "revolutions of rising entitlements" in the areas of civil rights, political rights, and social rights. And these claims are made, primarily, on the government.

Beyond this, these claims are increasingly made on a "group basis." Demands are levied that disadvantaged groups—blacks, women, specified national minorities—be given quotas or preferential treatment. Only in that fashion, is it argued, can historical injustices be redressed.

4. A Public Ethos.   The rising concern in recent years with "the quality of life" may well reflect a better-educated public, which has become more attentive to public issues. Another explanation is "the de Jouvenel paradox," which was first stated by the distinguished French social philosopher, Bertrand de Jouvenel. He observed that most persons find that, when their incomes are doubled, they don't live twice as well as before, and this is the source of disorientation and discontent in the new middle classes.[5] The reason is rooted in the further paradox that commodities the individual wants, and from which he derives a psychic gain, *in the aggregate* become a nightmare. The most obvious example is the automobile and traffic congestion. Each individual finds the automobile a great source of personal mobility and freedom; but its massive use leads to frustration. This is multiplied in a dozen ways. We read of a past generation enjoying Yosemite Valley, the Riviera, or the Mexican beaches; but when thousands crowd those limited spaces, the sense of beauty and repose is destroyed. The resources of recreation, environment, air, water, and land are more limited than they were before—especially when their previous use was "free." And, inevitably, that sense of loss, which derives from the fact that life is not twice as good as before though one's income has doubled, gives rise to public demands for regulation of the environment.

REGULATION AS A
POLITICAL BARGAINING PROCESS

It is a characteristic American response to a perceived wrong to pass a law and to punish the culprit. We have not only regulated business but morals as well—the most comprehensive experiment being the 1919–33 experience with prohibition of the use of spirituous liquors. The degree of regulation of business life in the United States is quite awesome in its range and scope. Probably not one area of business activity today is untouched by some kind of government regulation. But the central question is not the efficacy of any particular agency or specific issue of regulation, but the regulatory process itself and its consequences for the corporation and for the society.

The naive view of the regulatory process, as A. Myrick Freeman and Robert Haveman have pointed out, is that the governmental agency establishes rules and regulations to govern the behavior of the regulated firms and to promote the public interest. The reality is quite different. Regulation/enforcement is essentially a political process entailing bargaining between parties of unequal power. Sometimes the greater power is in the hands of the regulatory agency, sometimes in the hands of business. Louis Jaffe, of Harvard Law School, has probably stated the situation most accurately: The agencies are not so much industry-oriented or consumer-oriented as *regulation-oriented*. They are in the regulation business and regulate they will, with or without a rationale. The public interest is diffuse, poorly organized and poorly represented, and often comes out second or third best.[6]

A CHAOTIC POLITICAL SYSTEM

A second problem is the chaotic nature of the political system. In a pithy observation, Samuel Huntington has pointed out that the United States has, perhaps, the most *modern economy* in the world—flexible, adaptive, and product-oriented. At the same time, it has a Tudor polity, with administrative structures—counties, townships, municipalities—that are in no way responsive to the "fields of force" of the economic and political issues they have to confront. Problems are shifted from the federal to the state to the local governments, and vice versa, or from the legislature to the bureaucracy, mainly to avoid accountability or the resolution of public-policy conflicts. In the end, one has in many areas—and water pollution is a case in point—piecemeal, fragmented decisions which serve the public poorly.

And finally, as a result of all this, one has an "overload" of burdens on the political system which impedes its functioning, creates heavy tax and administrative burdens, and leads to despair by all concerned about the ability of the society to handle its problems.

THE SHIFT FROM MARKET
TO POLITICAL DECISIONS

One of the fundamental structural changes that has taken place in American society, in great measure because of the onrush of communal problems, is a shift from market to political decisions. The virtues of the market are many. It is an affair of many buyers and many sellers, each insistent upon getting his own terms; and if either is not satisfied, he can go elsewhere and seek to do better. From a societal point of view, the central virtue of the market is that it "disperses" responsibility. If du Pont introduces Corfam, and finds that the public will not buy it, the loss is its own. If there is a change in buying habits so that a particular industry loses jobs (as did the textile industry a decade ago because of a change in marriage age and the adoption of a suburban lifestyle), there is "nobody" to blame. But in political decision making, the situation is reversed. The decision points are visible and it is clear whose ox will be gored. Where to locate a jetport or a generating plant, or whether a freeway will go through the ghetto or the rich section of town, are all decisions made at "city hall." Everybody organizes and goes down to fight. The result is an increase in community conflict and in the politics of "stymie."

And yet, public control of business is inescapable. The fundamental argument was laid down forty years ago by the distinguished economist John Maurice Clark:

> The frontiers of control are expanding. They are expanding geographically, increasing the importance of national functions as compared with those of local governments and compelling the beginnings of international regulation. And they are expanding in the range of things covered and the minuteness of regulation. . . . Whether one believes government control to be desirable or undesirable, it appears fairly obvious that the increasing interdependence of all parts of the economic system . . . will force more control in the future than has been attempted in normal times in the past.[7]

The relevant issues are the definitions of the public interest and the public purpose. The relevant strategy is to minimize administrative and bureaucratic regulation, and to utilize the market mechanism to achieve those purposes. In the case of pollution, for example, we can use an "economic-incentives" approach, which would force the "culprit" to internalize the costs he has generated or to pay for them through a tax penalty. The point is that air and water have been "free goods"; and when any goods have no cost there is little incentive to economize on their use; and we have paid for this in the spoliation of the environment. By assessing the true economic cost to the polluter, we provide an incentive for him to use the resource with care.[8]

As David Hume pointed out two-hundred years ago, we live in a "political society," in which the most obvious problems arise in achieving social cooperation. "Two neighbors," he said, "may agree to drain a meadow which they possess in common, because it is easy for them to know each other's mind, and each must perceive . . . the immediate consequence of his failing in his part. . . . But it is very difficult . . . that a thousand persons should agree in any such action, it being difficult for them to concert so complicated a design . . . and each seeks a pretext to free himself of the trouble and expense and would lay the whole burden on others."

A political society, necessarily, implies a common public philosophy and an agreement on procedures to fulfill its purposes. For almost two-hundred years, there has been in this country an "implicit consensus" that sought to realize the goals of individual freedom within the

framework of the common welfare. Each social problem and each political act is a test of that consensus. The problems that we confront challenge the historic consensus that has guided this society. And the perils
of failure are great. Our response as a nation has been, too often, "too
late and too much." The question is whether we can find better
answers—in time.

NOTES

1.   Abram Chayes, "The Modern Corporation and the Rule of Law," in
The Corporation in Modern Society, ed. Edward S. Mason (Cambridge, Mass.:
Harvard University Press, 1959), p. 26.

2.   As Mr. Brewster commented further, in a prescient statement:

> No doubt arming a dealer with the power of legal complaint if his franch-
> ise is terminated without cause flies in the face of competition's traditional
> reliance on freedom of customer selection and rejection. But if the laws
> designed to enforce competition cannot prevent centers of dependence, if
> bargain has to such an extent given way to ultimatum, then other avenues
> of redress will be found.

"The Corporation and Economic Federalism," in Mason, *The Corporation,* p. 77.

3.   From *U.S. Statistical Abstract, 1971,* table 76, p. 57.

4.   The *Comstock* case, as well as the negligence of the auto industry on
safety, are thoroughly documented in two significant essays by Daniel P.
Moynihan, "Traffic Safety and the Body Politic," and "The Automobile and the
Courts," in *Coping: On the Practice of Government* (New York: Random House,
1973).

5.   To that extent, the Jouvenel paradox can join "the Tocqueville effect"
in explaining the nature of social turmoil. Tocqueville, it may be recalled, in his
study of the French Revolution, remarked that it is not when things go from
better to worse but from worse to better that a revolutionary situation is more
likely to occur, because individuals who have no hope for change become
apathetic, whereas those who see an opportunity become impatient—the
source, thus, for the idea of the revolution of rising expectations.

6.   For a summary of the MacAvoy and Jaffe arguments, plus some
pungent statements of his own, see James Q. Wilson, "The Dead Hand of Regulation," *The Public Interest,* no. 25 (Fall 1971). Also see, A. Myrick Freeman and
Robert Haveman, "Clean Rhetoric and Dirty Water," *The Public Interest,* no. 28
(Summer 1972).

7.   John Maurice Clark, "Government Regulation of Industry,"
Encyclopedia of the Social Sciences (New York: Macmillan, 1932), 7:129.

8.   For a detailed argument on how this would work, see Freeman and
Haveman, "Clean Rhetoric and Dirty Water," and Lawrence J. White, "The
Auto Pollution Muddle," *The Public Interest,* no. 32 (Summer 1973).

THE DYNAMICS OF LEGITIMACY

Kenneth E. Boulding

EXCHANGE AND THREAT AS INSTITUTIONAL BASES

Governments and businesses represent two genera of the social-ecological system. Each of the genera contains species such as corporations, partnerships, and proprietorships in the case of businesses; world, federal, state, and local bodies in the case of governments. Then we have the hybrids between them, such as the Tennessee Valley Authority, the Port of New York Authority, COMSAT, Amtrak, or the U.S. Postal Service. What we have is a spectrum of organizational forms, so that it is by no means easy to tell where government ends and business begins. At the extremes of the spectrum we are pretty sure that the United States is a government and General Motors is a business.

In capitalist societies the main distinction is that businesses exist primarily in an exchange environment and survive because what they sell has a greater value in the market than its cost. In exchange there is neither obligation nor duty, and either seller or buyer in a potential exchange has a veto that can be exercised without fear of any sanctions, moral or material.

Governments, by contrast, even though they do buy and sell, operate in an environment that might be described as one of legitimated threat. Their income is derived mainly from taxes rather than from voluntary exchange; and most people pay their taxes to avoid serious trouble.

Even the distinction between exchange and threat, however, is not wholly clear. There is, again, a spectrum that runs through various forms and degrees of obligation and duty: From "I must buy from this store because the owner is my friend"; or "I must give to charity or else I will feel mean;" toward "I must pay my taxes because if I don't I will be put in jail."

Both exchange and threat, however, must be regarded as legitimate by the parties concerned if they are to be effective in organizing social systems. An illegitimate threat, like that of a bandit, may organize a small temporary social system. An illegitimate exchange, as in the black market, can only organize small-scale systems. Large organized social systems, however, always require legitimacy, and legitimacy is perhaps the most important single dynamic element in the social system, although probably the least understood. If an institution or organization loses legitimacy, it may operate for a while in the underground, but the probability of its survival is severely reduced. Legitimacy, unfortunately, is not easy to measure; but that it is a major driving force in social dynamics can hardly be doubted.

THE NATURE OF LEGITIMACY

Legitimacy has two fundamental aspects: internal and external. *Internal* legitimacy is almost equivalent to morale. It represents a conviction on the part of people occupying roles in an organization that what they are doing is "OK." Legitimacy indeed could almost be defined as "OK-ness." Without this internal legitimacy no person or organization could continue to function for very long, for the springs of action would be corroded. *External* legitimacy is the conviction on the part of other persons or organizations that the organization or person in question is OK.

Legitimacy, however, is divisible; some aspects or some actions of the person or organization may be regarded as legitimate while others may not. A conscientious objector, for instance, denies legitimacy to the government's act of conscription, but does not necessarily deny legitimacy to other acts of government. We may deny legitimacy to a business that bribes politicians or engages in shady deals, but do not necessarily withdraw legitimacy from the business institution. Sometimes, however, there is a total withdrawal of legitimacy, as in revolutions, or when people withdraw from roles, for instance, by quitting or retiring, or are forcibly removed from them by firing or a failure to be reelected. The moment a term of a president expires, for instance, he is no longer legitimate if he tries to operate in that office. We could very well argue that it is the role that is legitimate rather than the person. There is, indeed, an important distinction between the legitimacy of the occupant and the legitimacy of the role. We may deny legitimacy to the occupant at the same time that we accord legitimacy to the role, as, for instance, when we try to impeach a president.

LEGITIMACY IN
BUSINESS-GOVERNMENT RELATIONS

In the complex interactions between businesses and governments, the shifting assets of legitimacy play a dominant role. The relationship is a little one-sided. There may be something like exchange and exchange-oriented organizations even in primitive societies, which are almost leaderless, without anything that could really be called a government. The invention of coinage, however, represented a sharp intervention of government into the exchange system, for if a government issues coins, this imposes a stamp of legitimacy on money. Merchants,

especially international traders, have always existed with slightly dubious legitimacy, in the cracks of the system. In the search for legitimacy
they have sometimes sought protection from powerful governments, or
even set up governments of their own, as in the medieval city-states.

The legitimation of exchange and of organizations based on it,
however, cannot simply be taken for granted. It is something that developed painfully in the course of social evolution, as, for instance, in
the very primitive form of "silent trade." If all men are enemies, as in
the Hobbesian state of nature, then obviously there can be no trade. It
is almost always regarded as illegitimate to trade with the enemy.

The corporation is a creature of government and derives its
legitimacy in part from the government that incorporates it. It is possible, of course, to form organizations without governments. There have
been many societies in which political and religious organizations have
existed side by side on relatively equal status, each perhaps granting a
certain legitimacy to the other. Some, indeed, argue that the relations
of government and business in the United States are like those of the
church and state in the Middle Ages, in the sense that it is hard to tell
who is the donor and who is the recipient of legitimacy. Certainly,
there is a very complex interaction.

SOURCES OF LEGITIMACY

There has not been a great deal of empirical research into the
dynamics and sources of legitimacy. In previous papers I have suggested a number of possible sources. The first, of course, is *positive
payoffs*. Institutions that are rewarding rather than punishing easily become legitimate, and after they are no longer rewarding they tend to
lose their legitimacy. The situation is enormously complicated, however, by the fact that *sacrifice* is also an important source of legitimacy,
and persons or institutions who are able to demand sacrifice of others
often achieve external legitimacy because of it. One reason is that sacrifice produces a sense of sacredness, and sacredness—an important
source of legitimacy—is often reinforced by sacrifice. Another reason is
that, once we have made sacrifices for anything, our identity becomes
involved with it and it is hard for us to admit that our sacrifices have
been in vain. This is the phenomenon I have called the "sacrifice trap,"
which is particularly important in understanding the different legitimacy profiles of business and government. Government has a quasi-
sacred character, which is constantly being refurbished by sacrifices
both of the taxpayer and, more fundamentally, of citizens. Businesses,
on the other hand, require very little sacrifice; they have to derive their
legitimacy almost wholly from the positive payoffs they produce—and
they have very little sacredness. This is, indeed, one of the major prob-

lems of legitimating institutions of exchange. Whereas institutions of the threat system, whether of church or state, easily acquire sacredness, the institutions of the exchange system have a kind of cruddy earthiness. It is hard to legitimate something that simply does very mild good, such as a bank.

Ambivalence is another powerful source of legitimation, as expressed in the approach-avoidance conflict noted by Neal Miller and Gregory Bates. We go towards and consume or absorb those objects that are merely attractive. We go away from those objects that are merely repulsive. Those with both qualities find us in a continuing and inescapable attachment.

Other sources of legitimation and delegitimation should be noted briefly. One is age; things that have been around for a long time acquire legitimacy from sheer habit. Another is consistency; inconsistent people or institutions tend to lose legitimacy. Another is credibility; being found out in telling a deliberate lie is a very powerful source of delegitimation, indeed, as a number of politicians and businessmen have discovered. There may be something of a paradox here. Being lied to and then being disillusioned is a form of suffering, which may actually engender legitimacy. In itself, however, disillusionment is a very powerful source of delegitimation; and trying to build legitimacy on detectable illusions is a very dangerous game, which has affected both government and business. One almost comes to the conclusion that the honest and unabashed imposition of sacrifice is the surest way to gain legitimacy!

THE DYNAMICS OF LEGITIMACY

Another interesting subject is the legitimacy of particular interactions. Certain exchanges, for instance, are regarded as legitimate in most societies, while others are not. In our own society slavery is a form of exchange that is extremely illegitimate; prostitution has dubious legitimacy; whereas buying at the supermarket is totally legitimate. Certain government interventions in business may be regarded as legitimate, others as illegitimate; and the line often shifts for reasons that are not always clear. In the United States, for instance, we saw a marked shift towards the legitimacy of certain forms of government intervention, such as antitrust legislation in the late nineteenth century; then we accepted another shift in the direction of more direct intervention as a result of the Great Depression.

The role of rhetoric in legitimation-delegitimation is a very tricky and difficult problem, but one of great importance. Why, for instance, did the Marxist rhetoric fall on such receptive ears in Eastern Europe and in Russia, whereas in Western Europe and the United States it has remained relatively ineffective? Similarly, the rhetoric of free private enterprise is effective at one time and less effective at another. An analysis of these rhetorical systems is very much overdue. The only difficulty is that we don't have good theoretical foundations for analyses of these kinds, and, particularly, we seem to lack an adequate theory of persuasion and argument. Speech and communications departments may know something about rhetoric, but the theory is still rather obscure.

The study of legitimacy is, of course, far beyond the ordinary competence of economists. If we had to classify it at all, perhaps we should regard it as social anthropology, as it underlies so many economic problems, decisions, and policies. Some interdisciplinary activity in this direction could very well be fruitful. What we look forward to in the future is an extraordinarily complex network of interacting legitimacies, some rising, some declining. Merely listing them illustrates the complexity of the problem.

Thus, on the government side we have:

1. The declining legitimacy of *war*, as reflected, for instance, in war songs. As wars have been a major function of governments, this has led to a general decline in the respect for the legitimacy of government, which is seen in the United States at the moment.
2. The declining legitimacy of *inequality*. The demand for equality, however, can be met only by a public grants economy, which necessitates a favorable attitude toward the legitimacy of government. These are conflicting forces and it is hard to say which is in the ascendant. There are strong pressures both for increase and for diminution of the public grants economy.
3. The legitimacy of political action as against *civil disobedience* or even armed revolt is a complex process going on in some parts of the world. This is bound up with the whole question of the legitimacy of violence and of other alternatives.

On the business side we have:

1. The legitimacy of *profits and interest,* and of nonlabor income in general. This is, of course, an old problem that is strongly related to the legitimacy of equality, because nonlabor income is always distributed much more unequally than is labor income. It is also related to feelings about reward according to deserts: "What has he done to get all this?"
2. The legitimacy of *calculatedness.* To be businesslike is to be calculating. But it is deemed good to be businesslike, and bad to be calculating.

3. The legitimacy of *work*. Alienation is supposed to result from work that is meaningless to the worker because it is too sub-divided. What leads people into alienated cultures (criminals, guerrillas, Weathermen, etc.) is very imperfectly understood.

There are also problems that cut across the business-government distinction, for instance, the legitimacy of large-scale versus small-scale organizations, or of bureaucratic versus participatory power structures. Sorting all these crosscurrents out is an intellectual task that still waits to be performed.

BUSINESS AND GOVERNMENT:
THE WALLS BETWEEN

L. Earle Birdzell

The government of the modern state has become an active partner in the management of the modern economy—and from some points of view, the senior partner. The role of monetary and fiscal policy in maintaining a stable, full-employment economy implies a continuous government role in a fundamental aspect of economic life. Some of the politicization of economic decision making derives from this commitment to full employment. More politicization occurs simply because a working political majority no longer sees any serious objection to using political power to change an unpopular market outcome. There are other factors; but the result is that government and business meet each other along a deep zone, where boundaries are poorly defined and readily changed in response to pragmatic demands. Such lawless border marches always breed guerrilla warfare.

BORDER WARFARE
BETWEEN GOVERNMENT AND BUSINESS

It may be a maverick opinion that this border warfare has so far been more damaging to government than to business. Assuming responsibilities it could not meet, in responding to expectations no one knows how to fulfill, while neglecting its historically prior duties, overloaded government at all levels has suffered a drop in public confidence amounting to collapse.[1]

Not that business has escaped real injury. The most serious damage probably results from a combination of tax, price control, and antitrust policies, which deter the sophisticated investor from putting his money into American manufacturing industry. And the political community has effectively persuaded a large segment of the public that the business community is responsible for the easily predictable (and freely predicted) adverse consequences of governmental policy actions. The two most conspicuous recent instances are, of course, inflation and energy. It is fair to add that, businessmen, qua border guerrillas, do not have the satisfaction of having inflicted any of their adversaries' wounds. Businessmen have lost all the battles; government's failures are primarily attributable to the limitations of its own processes.

There is no consensus that this border war should cease. Peace with victory requires a painful choice of victor; and this is probably one of those wars nobody should win. But a peace of compromise is not clearly the answer. Cooperative relationships between business and government recall the controversial implications of the phrase, "military-industrial complex." And there are those who look upon separation of economic power from political power as fundamental to the survival of political democracy. As usual, the way of the peacemaker promises to be hard.

Suppose, nevertheless, that we assume for purposes of argument that government and business institutions—in common with the other institutions of our society—ought to work together actively in the pursuit of the national welfare. On the assumption that some improvement in business-government relationships is desirable, we can ask: What is the structure of the relationships we are trying to improve? And what are some of the major stumbling blocks to their improvement?

A TOPOLOGY OF
BUSINESS-GOVERNMENT RELATIONSHIPS

In a sense, research in business-government relations is an effort to find something useful about R in the expression $R\ (g,\ b)$, where g stands for government organizations, b for business organizations, and R for some appropriate relationship. It is a large field.

The g variable of the relationship is plural and complex. Recent unsuccessful attempts to bring the federal bureaucracy under White House control should dispel any lagging illusions that the national government is a monolithic hierarchy. It turns out to be a loosely federated plurality of fiefdoms (sometimes called agencies or departments), each with a substantial degree of autonomy based on the strength of its own political constituency. Even without taking account of local government, the pluralism of g is clear.

And on the business side, the thought that "corporate capitalism" is something less than a completely coherent community will come as no surprise to anyone who still preserves the capacity to make distinctions. Both g and b are variables covering a broad range of specifics. Table 1—with no attempt at exhausting the universe—suggests the variety on both sides of R.

As to R itself, Table 2 shows one way to get a pictorial image of the plurality of relationships by making a profile for each of the government organization-business organization pairs shown in Table 1. This illustrative profile is one perception of the DOD-defense contractor relationship. Other individuals and relationships will produce different profiles. Just to complicate matters, if R turns out to be asymmetrical, R $(b,\ g)$ would have a different profile from $R\ (g,\ b)$:

TABLE 1

Government Organizations	Related Business Organizations
Department of Defense National Aeronautics and Space Administration	Defense-space contractors
Department of Agriculture	Farmers; dairy, meat processors
Environmental Protection Agency	Auto manufacturers; electric utilities
Office of Energy Policy	Oil, coal companies
Securities and Exchange Commission	Brokers; underwriters; issuers
Interstate Commerce Commission	Railroads; truckers
Federal Communications Commission	Radio and TV stations; radio and TV networks; cable and pay TV
U.S. Tariff Commission	Trade unions; businesses subject to import competition
Food and Drug Administration	Drug industry; food and beverage manufacturers
Federal Reserve Board Council of Economic Advisers Treasury Department Cost of Living Council	Banks; general businesses; unions
Federal Power Commission	Electric utilities; natural gas producers
Nuclear Regulatory Commission	Atomic energy equipment builders
Antitrust Division Federal Trade Commission	Business in general

TABLE 2

Characterization of Relationship	INTENSITY OF CHARACTERIZATION				
	Substantially Absent	Perceptibly Present	Strongly Present	Dominant	Overwhelming
Symbiotic					●
Supportive				●	
Retardant	●				
Protective			●		
Exploitive		●			
Adversary		●			

Business-government relationships are irretrievably plural and diverse. Any new edifice of government-business collaboration will inevitably be built one step at a time, by different people working in different specialties. Without invading the domain of these specialists, a generalist can only hope to touch on one or two background causes of the frictions associated with the specific manifestations of R.

THE CLASH OF ETHICAL SYSTEMS:
INDIVIDUALISM VERSUS COLLECTIVISM

Proust thought that nothing separates two men more than adherence to differing ethical systems. If he was right, the separation between government and business is not hard to understand.

An ethical system has to reconcile individual self-interest with that degree of consideration of others necessary to keep peace within the community. But the demands of an ethical system may range from the minimum necessary to community survival up to the maximum consistent with individual survival. These polarities set up two different ethical systems—individualist and collectivist—and we usually end with a mixture of the two.

The ethical system of the business world makes maximum concessions to self-interest. With rare exceptions, an individual is not expected to buy, sell, accept a job, hire an employee, save or invest, except as he sees his own self-interest in doing so.[2] Although it would be wrong to underemphasize the many circumstances in which business ethics require actions out of organizational loyalty, contractual duty, or personal good faith, the basic appeal of the business organization to its investors, customers, and employees is: "We offer you as an individual more than any of our competitors offer you." No other social institution makes so simple an appeal to individual self-interest.

Government, on the other hand, claims the loyalty and support of its subjects on a wholly involuntary basis. The ethics of patriotism require a subordination of individual goals and self-interest to group goals and group self-interest.[3] The utilitarian ethics of the business community require the individual to sacrifice his immediate self-interest only peripherally, reluctantly, and rarely. But the modern state requires of the members of its bureaucracy the subordination of individual goals and self-interest to the general good as the central theme of life and career. The same kind of self-abnegation, in favor of the public good, is expected of all who would participate in politics by running for elective office.

This difference of ethical orientation is old. The civil servants of Germany, Britain, Sweden, and France, for example, have long esteemed themselves as "better people" than the money grubbers "in trade." What is new is the variety of the interrelationships that are heated up by the ethical differences between the civil service and business.

The state-oriented collectivist ethic is not limited to those in government. By and large, any government-operated system of education seeks to inculcate a government, rather than a business, ethical system. The teacher, being under the strongest of social obligations to instill subordination of self in favor of the community, is well-advised not to confuse the educational process by offering the student a choice between competing ethical traditions—at least not until the student has been irreversibly conditioned!

Educational conditioning is abetted by the considerable persuasion our religious institutions can still bring to bear. One does not go to church to be told to cultivate one's own selfish preferences. From Jeremiah to the present, the admonition is to charge everyman's conscience with everyman's ills. And no one gets moral credit for benefiting others if he benefits himself in the process.

By and large, the arts and the media also reflect a preference for a collectivist ethic. In theory, artists may be assumed to attach importance to the right to individuality. Yet their views of people who achieve individuality by becoming rich are rarely flattering. Working members of the media cannot even afford a high regard for the right to individuality, associated as it is with a corresponding regard for privacy. Besides, to survive economically they must address themselves to a mass audience.

Nevertheless, the individualist ethic has an ancient and respectable lineage. With modest allowance for the passing of 2,300 years, the modern businessman could read with pleasure the description of the individual virtues in the *Nicomachean Ethics*.[4] Bertrand Russell ridiculed Aristotle's picture of the "great-souled" man for requiring a personal wealth and cultured leisure unattainable by modern democratic man.[5] But he had not anticipated post-World War II affluence, which made the Athenian ideal something not too far from a feasible goal for many in democratic societies.

The individual ethic is also the ethic of personal freedom. What individual freedom is all about is minimizing the load of obligations society imposes on the individual. What collectivist ethics is all about is maximizing the obligations assumed by the individual and discouraging him from pursuing his own self-interest. The choice of ethical reference points is not advanced by the claim that societal restrictions on the freedom of some result in greater freedom for all. That gets out of ethics and into economics; and economics points to the opposite conclusion.

Many differences between business and government are traceable to the divergence of underlying ethical assumptions. These differences fester because ethical assumptions are not easily made the subject of rational dialogue. Almost by definition they are beyond reason. The adaptation of collectivist ethics to business is not an attractive solution. The individualist ethic is valuable as a check on the trend to the Orwell-Skinner society. And the business system would not work as well with a collectivist ethic. On the other hand, the adaptation of the business ethic to government, art, religion, education, or even the media is also not a feasible way out.

The ethical schism between business and government is only one of a whole set of societal gaps. Specialization in modern societies seems to generate clusters of subcultures, differing one from another in ethics, value systems, and goal structures. The differences between the business and public sectors are merely examples of this larger tendency toward a divided society and a multiplicity of sectors. A libertarian could afford to be relaxed about this tendency, except for two considerations. First, the separate sectors tend to develop their own insular xenophobias, and to form attitudes toward nearby subcultures compounded of distrust, envy, contempt, fear, and animosity. For any given subculture, others may be viewed as threats. Second, these attitudes generate barriers to effective communication, which may build up to the point where it becomes impossible to work out acceptable solutions to problems that must be solved by civilized people sharing the same geophysical—and psychological—space. No one knows quite what the Harris polls on loss of public confidence in institutions are really reflecting. One possible interpretation is that, as subcultures multiply and dominate, trust and confidence across their boundaries are even harder for the pollsters to find.[6]

The collectivist ethic emphasizes the *equality* of individuals. Equality in a religious and in a political sense—before God and the law—is a generally held ideal. Educational institutions have a more ambiguous attitude; effective teacher-pupil relationships have proved resistant to the equalizing process, and the practice of grading the pupils still prevails. But there is nothing ambiguous about the business attitude. A major objective of business is to discover, highlight, magnify, exploit, and reward or punish all of the individual *in*equalities that can be identified, with indifference to arguments about whether an inequality originates in the genetic endowment or in the environment. The business game is a standing challenge to the ideal of equality, and to the pragmatic value of deeply cherished egalitarian assumptions.

BUSINESS LACKS A POLITICAL CONSTITUENCY AND POLITICAL POWER

A relationship characterized by great power on one side and weakness on the other is not politically stable. People with negative attitudes toward business generally claim that the imbalance of power between government and business favors the business side. The truth is, however, that the business community is living—dangerously—in what amounts to a political power vacuum. Its political position might be compared to that of the goose that laid golden eggs: Most voters do not want to turn off the supply of eggs, but they are highly susceptible to all sorts of suggestions for reducing the cost of the care and feeding of the goose. The quantum of public sympathy and affection for this goose could be measured in a thimble.

The political weakness of business is probably traceable in great part to the ethical conflict just outlined. The utilitarian business ethic has only rarely been able to stir emotions and to rally a politically useful voting bloc to its cause.[7] Investors, employees, and customers have resisted political organization in behalf of business. Government can engage in political predation against, say, the oil industry, with no risk of any such adverse reaction as results from a like attack on the interests of firearm users, even though investors in, and employees of, the major oil companies must considerably outnumber the membership of the National Rifle Association.

A meaningful political power base requires both votes and money. In our affluent society, money is not likely to be lacking for any interest with a good-sized block of votes. It would be wrong to discourage businessmen from contributing to political candidates. But political contributions made in dissociation from deliverable votes may be anything from expressions of esteem to payments of blackmail. The one thing they are *not* is a source of political power. At most, the elected representative can afford to vote his contributor's way on issues that are politically neutral in his district; and such issues are not likely to have more than interstitial importance. And woe betide the political figure who pays his campaign debts in better coin.

For practical purposes, American business today has no political rights. True, burglary and embezzlement against a corporation are still crimes, but more to keep out interlopers and to preserve the goose intact for more formal exploitation than because of any governmental solicitude for the victim. Today, it is simply futile to challenge legislative or regulatory proposals relating to business organizations in terms of freedom of speech, freedom from unreasonable search and seizure, freedom of contract, freedom to engage in political activity, or even the right to a fair trial. This is not to get into the legal question of the applicability of these constitutional rights to corporations; but rather to note that only a near-total political power vacuum would have left the basic political liberties as irrelevant as they are. Today's corporation is not so much an artificial person as a nonperson!

The exercise of political power requires communication, and communication between government and business on significant national economic issues is today a land of almost pure fantasy. The submissions of business representatives to government are generally rejected on grounds of self-interest. The fact that gloomy business predictions about legislative proposals have a regrettably high percentage of confirmation by events is not considered relevant. A practicing politician can, as a rule, make a career of economic "reform" only by ignoring both business spokesmen and anyone in public office who has spent enough time in the business arena affected by the "reform" to be embarrassed by personal knowledge of the subject.[8]

The current substitutes for firsthand evidence from business are "experts" drawn from government, legislative staffs, academia, and private consulting firms. The weaknesses of the process are obvious, but it is still the only one we have for maintaining the surface conventions of rationality in dealings between business and government. Drawn as they are from a tradition of courtroom litigation, these expertizing procedures may be adequate to reach "go-no-go" judgments on some legislative proposals. They are obviously not an effective vehicle for mounting joint attacks on such problems as urban renewal, mass transportation, education of the disadvantaged, employment discrimination, energy supplies, rational taxation, inflation, pensions, medical care, and the like.

Another aspect of the political power vacuum is the general absence of political competence within business organizations, a fact that invites a research project. "Political competence" here means the ability to generate substantial voting support for a political position affecting the interests of the business organization, or for or against a candidate whose election would affect its interests. Certainly the exercise of political competence would require corporate managers to do a number of things for political, rather than business, reasons. The less burdensome course is to leave politics to the corporate specialists in *ex post* rationalization—those in public relations or law. In any case, there is seldom space in business organizations for demonstrated political competence.

The importance of a voting constituency arises from the fact that political proposals affecting business usually involve a substantial range of choice, from something reasonably acceptable to something downright poisonous. A legislative policymaker may wish to stop short of poisoning the goose. In fact, he may not want to hurt it at all. But whatever his intentions, it is much easier for the legislator to use his political skills to pick a politically safe stopping point than it is for him to use his economic skills to work through the expert evidence to a scientifically safe stopping point. The one legitimate power base for "getting a good bill" is a voting constituency. The attempt to protect the political interests of the corporation, without a voting constituency, produces the appearance of both incompetence and corruption. Without the legitimate power base, only the rare genius among corporate lobbyists will emerge otherwise than ineffective, frustrated, inept, discouraged, corrupt, or some combination of the five.

THE FUTURE RELATIONSHIP IN A
MATURE URBAN SOCIETY

Societies survive because crises that need to be resolved *are* regularly resolved. Another reason for expecting business-government relationships to improve is that business organizations are, by general agreement based on much evidence, the most adaptable institution yet invented.

There also may be another source of hope. Some regions, particularly in the Midwest, have experienced virtually no population growth and no substantial inward migration during the last fifty years. The public schools have had two generations in which to integrate and to assimilate the people who were there, and the process is very far along. The original ethnic neighborhoods are breaking up. At least to the casual observer, what emerges is a mature society, with low social tensions, a relaxed, optimistic population, and few signs of the social phenomena that invite characterizations drawn from the vocabulary of mental illness.

A similar experience on a national scale is overdue. The effects of cutting off large-scale foreign immigration after World War I have been delayed by the countereffects of the migration of rural populations to urban areas, and by the process of overturning old patterns of racial discrimination. Nevertheless, this migration, too, is finite. Within the next few decades we should find out whether a society can be both urban and democratic.[9]

With luck, the forces making for societal maturity will overbalance the forces making the disintegration. Business organizations will adapt to the process—perhaps even hurry it along. In so doing, they may alter the utilitarian ethic, but probably not very much. It is urban man that is inheriting the American earth; and urban man is, after all, a past master at the art of dealing with others on a basis where mutual self-interest is an implicitly required underwriter of trustworthiness. In short, the values of the business community may be closer to those of urban man than to those of rural man. The need for individual identity, coherent with the individualism of the business ethic, may well be more passionately felt in an urbanized than in a rural America. Business organizations just may acquire political constituencies or, more likely, have constituencies thrust upon them as the snowballs thrown at "the corporations" land on less abstract targets.

The needed research is, again, nonapocalyptic. The *R*s have to be taken one at a time, like the work of Sam Peltzman on the effects of drug legislation.[10] The list of candidates for the Peltzman technique is endless. Today, academic research in the social sciences is crowded with work aimed at stimulating the *next* attempt at overloading government. Measuring the results from the *old* attempts offers a wide-open field for new digging tomorrow.

NOTES

1. See Aaron Wildavsky, "Government and the People," *Commentary*, (1973) p. 25; and "Governmental performance depends . . . on selecting problems government knows how to solve." p. 28.

2. A current account unconsciously illustrating the two ethical systems in collision appears in an article by A. J. Keeffe and Paul Tierney:

> On July 30 William E. Simon, chairman of the President's Oil Policy Committee, by letter requested a meeting with Lewis A. Engman, chairman of the FTC, to discuss the oil situation and to offer his comments on the FTC study on which the proposed complaint is based. Mr. Simon stated that some oil companies that had announced plans for new refineries are now having second thoughts because of the threat of divestures and that the FTC action could have an adverse effect on the energy supply. To the FTC, however, this smacked of economic blackmail.

"Those Integrated Oil Companies: Is A Breakthrough Coming?" *American Bar Association Journal* (December 1973) 59: 1444.
Is this elementary good sense in appraising investment risks, or "economic blackmail?"

3. "Group goals and group self-interest" is, of course, a phrase of debatable ontological standing. The confirmed individualist can argue that it is a nonsense expression.

4. Consider, for example, the definition of virtue as a "mean, determined by reason, and as the man of practical wisdom would determine [1107a]; and the discussions of the individual virtues in Books III and IV, particularly "perfected self-mastery" [1117b–19b] and "great mindedness" [1123a–25a]. A less-taxed generation would appreciate also the discussion of "magnificence" [1122a–23a]. (Page references are to the marginal pagination in the *Everyman Edition* of the Smith-Ross translation of Aristotle's work.)

5. See Bertrand Russell, *A History of Western Philosophy* (New York: Simon & Schuster, 1945), pp. 172–84, *esp.* pp. 175–76.
Russell, a good egalitarian and a firm believer in charging the "comfortable" with other people's sufferings, found the *Ethics* "*repulsive*" [173], "smug" [174], and "useful to comfortable men of weak passions" [174].

6. This point of view is due in great part to Allan Janik and Stephen Toulmin, who described this kind of society as "Kakania"—a term that merits far greater currency than it has received. *Wittgenstein's Vienna* (New York: Simon & Schuster, 1973).

7.   The thought goes back to Schumpeter's *Capitalism, Socialism and Democracy* (New York: Harper, 1942); and was well-expressed by Kenneth Arrow in a short "op-ed" article:

> It is fear of many conservative thinkers, the late Joseph Schumpeter being perhaps the best known and most thorough-going and Irving Kristol being the latest, that the ideological commitment to capitalism is too weak to resist the idealistic appeal of socialism or similar doctrines, which promise a daily contribution to the common good.

The New York Times March 26, 1973, p. 39. "Somehow it has Overcome."

8.   The problem is that useful economic inventions tend to originate with people who have the advantage of living with the problems they solve—e.g., the chain store, the mail-order house, the department store, the integrated manufacturing company, assembly-line production, parts interchangeability, national marketing, the multinational corporation, stockholder-oriented systems of executive compensation, the institutional investor, etc. The political path to economic progress has a history of producing nonsolutions to what may even be nonproblems; the exceptions are far fewer than they should be.

9.   See "The Metropolis and Mental Life," in *The Sociology of Georg Simmel,* ed. Kurt Wolff (New York: Free Press, Macmillan, 1964) pp. 402–24.

10.   See Sam Peltzman, *Regulation of Pharmaceutical Innovation: The 1962 Amendments* (Washington, D.C.: American Enterprise Institute for Public Policy Research, June 1974).

TECHNOLOGICAL CHANGE
AND BUSINESS-GOVERNMENT RELATIONSHIPS

Simon Ramo

Accelerating technological developments increasingly constitute a major cause, and a key element in the solution, of our nation's socioeconomic problems. They point the way to new tasks, new opportunities, and new potentialities. The future will witness the forming of novel organizational teamings of governments with such private institutions of our society as business corporations, universities, and the professions. A new "socioindustrial complex" will emerge to attack the problems of the future in response to the insistent demands of the American people.

Let us consider some of the leading contemporary problems of social engineering. Among them are urban development and redevelopment, mass rapid transit, national self-sufficiency in energy, control of environmental pollution, broad medical care for all, and good housing for all population groups. As the popular demand for attention to these problems becomes louder and better articulated, the political pressures for action rise. We can make headway in meeting these demands if we apply our intellectual and physical resources more fully. And doing things right rather than wrong on the social engineering front brings not only social gain but also economic payoff, with a good return on the investment.

However, in each of these problem areas, we quickly run into the obstacle of inadequate organization. Our society does not now possess effective organizational structures and processes for setting goals, analyzing alternatives, selecting a preferred approach, deciding who shall execute it, how it will be paid for, or what the rules will be. A confused and changing business-government relationship is part of the difficulty; but it is only one constraining factor. A wave of organizational innovation will have to come.

PROVIDING MASS RAPID TRANSIT

Let us consider the problem of urban mass transit facilities. A typical resident of a typical large American city lives ten miles from his work, with no choice to live closer because of the city's "design." He drives this ten miles at an average of ten miles an hour, polluting the air as he goes, losing patience in the traffic, using up too much energy, and leaving his investment to stand all day in a parking lot. There is no rapid transit he can use instead. (The same scenario applies to his family's needs, whether they be to get to school, visit health care facilities, do shopping, or engage in recreation.) Tired before he even starts, he does thirty hours of work, and takes sixty hours to do it, portal to portal. This 2-to-1 ratio in potential economic payoff is sinful to ignore, even if we forget the petroleum supply problem.

But not just any "mass rapid transit" will capture a large part of this payoff. A transportation system representing a really sound return on investment is not merely a matter of vehicles and electronic controls. A viable system has to be designed into the total pattern of the city. It has to match jobs and homes, education, crime control, health care, goods distribution, and waste removal. The city as it is and as it is desired to be is influenced by the transportation system.

Nor is it sufficient to arrive at sensible results by studying only one city. Many cities, large and small, must be analyzed to search out common system design concepts and to arrive at the right selection of components that can be standardized and produced in volume, in order to bring costs down. Experiments have to be run on many critical aspects that cannot be predicted from statistics and analyses. Half the population could be expected to alter its life pattern if really good urban transportation were available. So we are speaking of serving 100 million people with a corresponding $100 billion of design, planning, and construction costs. None of our largest corporations could handle this size of investment, initial operating losses, and massive risk-to-return ratios.

If "mass rapid transit" is to happen, then a government-industry combine is needed. Only the government can perform the detailed analysis and planning for many cities, the setting of criteria, the making of socioeconomic trade-off decisions, the writing of specifications for the hardware, the sponsoring of the experiments, and the funding of much early prototype development. After that is done, private industry should be expected to participate and to invest in what then would appear to be a reasonable market potential from which a fair return on capital might be obtained. This will involve cooperative efforts among corporations, with full exchange of information and intimate teaming, in an effort to attain a position of strength. But the government will also be a participant, and will help to organize the teamwork. The government will be making decisions, even as it has been doing for decades on military projects, that will determine which private elements will reach successful operating positions in urban transportation.

CREATION OF NEW CITIES

Let us take another example—the creation of new cities. We need to accommodate 75 to 100 million more people in the next 25 years. Most will live in expanded existing cities. However, there may also be strong interest in creating new cities because of the benefits of a greatly improved urban life in cities started completely from scratch. We refer to the founding of a viable city where jobs, homes, schools, and hospitals constitute a harmonious interacting ensemble—a social and economic entity that did not previously exist.

For such a city of, say, 100,000 people, an investment of around $1 billion is required. To try to create such a new city solely as a government project would almost certainly lead to failure. Perhaps the project would never get off the ground, what with budget problems and political hassles. It is hard to imagine what incentives the government could provide that would persuade a private corporation to locate an important plant in such a city, putting its market position at the risk of on-again-off-again government bureaucratic approaches, and wondering whether employees could be enticed to live in a government town.

But are private approaches any more likely to succeed? We should not overlook the attractiveness of a potential billion-dollar capital gain on the land value resulting from the creation of a city of 100,000 people. That gain is the added price the market would put on land when occupied by 100,000 people who have banded together to enjoy social and economic interaction and cooperation. But again, we are up against huge start-up costs, prohibitive risk, and the long time needed for development. So a privately-developed project would require a *group* of very large corporations working closely with one another. It is not evident that present antitrust concepts would allow such a venture.

A third approach would be a combination of government and private action—government-influenced, government-regulated, and government-sponsored. Perhaps undeveloped federal land could be made available at a low price, with state and local governments providing such legislative actions or administrative rules as would ensure the new city's access to water, electric power, and transportation. Government would also have to see to fairness, civil liberties, and freedom from monopolistic and anticompetitive activities, while at the same time being a participant in deciding which companies will be allowed to take the risks and pocket the profits, and what relationships they would have with one another and with the government. The government would be half "doer" and half "policeman."

REDUCTION OF POLLUTION

Let us shift to a pollution example. Private industry is not likely to depollute the Mississippi or the Great Lakes simply as profit-seeking ventures. Currently, there is no large market for clear water. But the citizens will insist on clean water and ways will be found to provide it. The President of the United States could announce, for instance, as

President Kennedy did in 1961 with regard to the lunar landing project, that "we shall depollute the Great Lakes before the end of this decade." He would automatically be committing tens of billions of dollars to another program, one far more difficult than Apollo, involving, in addition to scientific experiments and technological advances, a host of socioeconomic parameters. How are the Great Lakes to be depolluted, and to what extent? What is the tradeoff between limiting the economic growth of cities around the Great Lakes and having relatively pure lake water? How shall we divide the burden among the cities, the utilities, transportation companies, and industrial firms? The search for answers would disclose new truths—but also mistakes, dead ends, and a sense of incompleteness and arbitrariness. The work itself would affect the rest of the country, and even other parts of the world with which the economy around the Great Lakes competes.

Sooner or later we shall probably engage in such mammoth environmental improvement projects. Even if the projects turn out to be smaller—the depollution of a section of a river, a modest lake, or a localized ocean bay area—they will involve the same elements. These are: government leadership, sponsorship, and participation in research and development; systems studies, the setting of goals, criteria, and controls; and the teaming of government, science, technology, and industry.

Here we note certain similarities to the handling of large-scale military problems. When it became clear to the American people that their security might be at stake, government, industry, and science were teamed. The government was in the role of a prime mover, sponsor, participant, and captain of the team. In responding to a government-announced military requirement, American business corporations team up to create what they see as the strongest combination—one that will win the privilege of doing the job against what they hope will be weaker competitive teams seeking the same contract. On one project, two or three large companies may be rivals, each seeking to best the other in learning as much as possible about the job and proposing superior technological, organizational, and economic answers. On another project, perhaps coming a little later or in parallel, these same competitors may join to pool their know-how and creativity in an effort to defeat other combines of lesser strength.

ENERGY SUPPLIES

We can see this point more clearly as we consider the nation's need for electrical energy. Unprecedented increases in generating capacity are being scheduled to meet population growth and the growth of energy per capita. At the same time we are determined to exert severe controls on the polluting of the environment, and we are facing a shortage of fuels. It is no longer a simple matter of individual companies competing to sell equipment to generate the required energy. The government now enters to set criteria, to determine the tradeoffs, to set allocations of fuel. It influences trends in the use of nuclear fuel as compared with conventional fossil fuels. The location of generating plants now constitutes a key environmental parameter under governmental control. Thus, government will influence the relative prices of competing approaches and determine the time-scheduling and implementation of development. Government money to advance new techniques becomes essential to a far different degree than would otherwise be the case. This applies, for example, to the "breeder" reactors. It also is exemplified by government-financed basic research on controlled thermonuclear fusion, which has the potential to provide all the electric power we (or any nation) could ever use with fuel that can be obtained from sea water.

As the energy and materials crises increasingly burden the United States, the government is going to be involved in a far broader way than preventing monopoly and assuring adequate competition among private participants. What the government does will determine the nature of activity by competitive private institutions.

INFORMATION TECHNOLOGY

Let us go now to an area of technology that many believe will have the greatest impact of all on our society over the next several decades. This is "the information technology revolution." It amounts to creating synthetic electronic brainpower, providing mass memory, and making available a vast capacity to handle information: to collect it, process it, disseminate it, communicate it over great distances, present it in new forms, correlate it, store it, and deliberate on it. Information is what makes the world go 'round. The fullest implementation of information technology will associate each of us—in our homes, businesses, professional work, hospitals, schools—with new electronic apparatus as commonly as we are now associated with the telephone and the automobile.

Synthetic brainpower must be one of the greatest boons to mankind that technology could ever bestow. With the electronic partner handling the high-capacity, mundane information duties, the human partner can rise to new heights of creative and socially advancing endeavors. But there are some constraints that will defer our realization of this potential rise in the society's intellect. For one thing, the changeover required in the way we handle all of our endeavors is fundamental in nature and tremendous in detail. The start-up costs are impressive. If almost everyone is associated with a $100-a-month device tied in to an information network, that means many billions of dollars for the terminal apparatus alone. Indeed, such information systems are not economically viable unless, as with television or the telephone, there are hundreds of millions of terminals in use.

But much more apparatus is required: the communication equipment between terminals, the satellites, the telephone lines and computers, the huge electronic libraries, and the central-station switching equipment. And then there is the "software"—the recorded programs, the available information that has to be formulated in electronic form and then continually updated and enhanced. To this add the design effort, and the production, installation engineering, and training. These call for more billions of dollars, reaching amounts well beyond the net worths of our largest corporations.

Interdisciplinary aspects are involved, and no one corporation possesses all the know-how needed. Suppose it were lawful for large corporations to come together to form huge combines to share the risk for such projects, and to couple their expertise. Imagine further that the team has a plan that tells it that, having invested such enormous amounts of money, taken so big a gamble, and waited for years until it is able to amortize the start-up costs, it can dominate the market. Then it is conceivable that this great boon to the society would occur relatively soon. Such a vast information-processing organization would undoubtedly be subjected to public utility regulation to prevent abuse of its monopoly power.

This advance will mature slowly *unless* (and I suggest this is probable) the government enters into the situation strongly. The government has substantial incentives to enter. Since it is the biggest organization, it handles more information than any other institution of our society. Also, already beginning to show itself, is a major social issue associated with information technology that will soon develop into a political problem. That issue is whether, as a result of the application of information technology to our way of life, we are going to have a robot society—a computer-controlled, regimented society—in which everything from pickle production to airplanes and jobs will be closely scheduled. With full use of advanced information technology, manufacturing firms can enjoy something close to "real-time" control of their operations, everything being optimized in timing and flow. It would be natural for corporations to tie together their information systems so that everything—material supply, production, marketing, distribution—can move most efficiently. Now, perhaps we can have a robot society!

If an information system can enter every nook and cranny of the economy and tell everyone what to do, where to be, and what to eat, then it can also offer to all citizens a well-described list of public policy alternatives. And it can enlist citizen participation in deciding what shall be produced and sold. The essence of free enterprise is the free market. With an information system operating, everyone who has an idea, who has a little capital to risk, could make immediate contact with his potential customers. You could merely step to the sophisticated electronic terminals in your home and respond to a commercial advertisement by pushing some buttons, thereby depleting your bank account electronically and adding an equal amount to that of the producer. Production and distribution could be electronically tied to orders. The entrepreneur would be in real-time market communication with his customer. There would be more efficient, less wasteful, less risky production. The competitive market system would become even more productive and responsive to consumer demands. Democratic decision making would become speedy and efficient.

Which of these two possibilities we get—the computerizied robot society or the participatory, democratic free-enterprise society—will be determined not by the technology but by the people. In the big new wave of information technology that threatens to engulf our society for good or evil, the government should be at the focal point of decision. It should referee, set standards, operate controls, and ensure privacy, protection, and fairness of opportunity. It should sponsor the system, captain the teams, make arrangements, order priorities, and set the rules.

INTERNATIONAL COOPERATION AND MULTINATIONAL BUSINESS

If we move to the international arena, then the points we are seeking to make by these examples seem to be enlarged. Many of the technological advancements turn out to be international in nature. Improved weather prediction and, ultimately, weather control, for example, will involve international cooperation, including technological matters, sponsorship, and science-industry teaming. The same is true for satellites in the sky, acting as artificial, signal-producing stars to make possible superior aircraft navigation and traffic control.

Satellite systems for observation, search, and assessment of the earth's resources constitute assets of interest to all nations. Such developments are unlikely to take place at a very rapid pace unless they include the many corporations in noncommunist nations who deal with these resources. Private efforts will have to be teamed with governments' efforts. Much the same can be said about the development of ocean resources, of new techniques for generating electrical energy, of the creation of substitutes for materials in limited supply over the earth's surface, or of control of the environment. Each requires international cooperation with new rules and regulations, and each requires multigovernmental sponsorship.

These international projects require cooperation between governments and multinational companies. Corporate home bases may be, of course, in different nations, each with its own types of controls, antitrust concepts, and attitudes toward the teaming of government and industry. The United States probably will continue to have an international balance-of-payments problem, the solution of which lies in substantial part in exploiting our technological leadership. American policies regarding multinational corporations, the teaming of corporations with government, and our attitude toward antitrust laws are all bound to be influenced by a growing need to ensure strong U.S. participation in the world technological arena.

THE HYBRID ECONOMY OF THE FUTURE

When government finds it necessary to enter so deeply into regulation of the economy as it has recently, then we must recognize that ours is not a free-enterprise economy. We have a *hybrid* economy of government control and free enterprise. Although we have never had *wholly* free enterprise in the United States, the existence of severe price controls during peacetime under a Republican Administration suggests that we are farther away from laissez faire than we have been in the last 200 years.

Government participation in the economy is here to stay. Technological change has forced upon the world, and particularly upon the United States, a much more complex and fast-moving society. Interrelationships among private groups and governments are now increasingly vital. The notion that government should stay out of problem-solving and should do the absolute minimum is obsolete.

But we must also abandon the equally narrow idea that equates "private interest" with evil, and concludes that everything must be done by government. What we have, and what we shall continue to have, is a hybrid economy. Accepting this basic premise, let us now invent organizational arrangements for meeting the problems of our times —arrangements that amount to a "socioindustrial complex," a teaming of government and industry with appropriate roles for each.

CHAPTER 3

Modes and Social Costs of Government Regulation of Business

That government regulation of business enterprises is widely thought to be a focal point of friction in U.S. business-government relationships is shown by the fact that four participants in the seminar chose to write on this theme. Their papers explore, in turn: (1) changing modes of governmental regulation, (2) the substantial—but little noted—costs of such regulation, (3) ways of extending market competition in lieu of bureaucratic regulation, and (4) guidelines for dealing with large firms and. concentrated industries under the antitrust laws. These papers stress the large hidden costs to the American people of civil servant regulation of the private sector, as against its regulation by the impersonal forces of competition in open markets. All of these authors express the belief that competition is—or can be made—an effective guardian of the public interest over many areas of the U.S. economy now constrained by the rules of government agencies.

John R. Meyer *describes changing fashions in government regulation, commencing with the joint public-private management agency, such as the Interstate Commerce Commission; continuing with the functional regulatory agency, such as the Federal Trade Commission or the Securities and Exchange Commission; and ending with joint public-private enterprises, such as the Federal National Mortgage Association or the Communications Satellite Corporation. Meyer concludes that there is a propensity to deterioration—a law of entropy—which governs regulatory agencies. He suggests that this might be counteracted by giving them a limited life, to be extended only if searching inquiry shows that their benefits exceed their costs to society. Meyer is the 1907 Professor of Transportation, Logistics, and Distribution in the Graduate School of Business Administration at Harvard University, and is also President of the National Bureau of Economic Research, Inc. His wide experience as chairman, consultant, or member of numerous government bodies dealing with transportation, environmental, and other economic problems exceptionally qualifies him to write on regulatory issues. He is author or coauthor of nine books and numerous articles.*

Roger G. Noll *presents a penetrating analysis of the social costs of the regulatory process, which he graphically defines as* Penncentralization *(impairing of incentives to operate efficiently),* Lockheedization *(subsidizing inefficient firms),* Legalization *(requiring endless red tape), and* Consultantization *(diverting scarce talent from the production to the redistribution of wealth). Finding that the traditional theory of regulation lacks validity, he describes a political-economic model of regulation, which displays a bias in favor of represented interests and a bias against innovation. Noll is Professor of Economics at California Institute of Technology, where he has served since 1965. Educated there and at Harvard University, he has been a senior staff economist on the President's Council of Economic Advisors. From 1970 to 1973 he was a codirector of the Brookings Studies in the Regulation of Economic Activity.*

Murray L. Weidenbaum *presents a new model of governmental decision making, in which government would use taxation and market prices instead of bureaucrats and regulatory agencies to achieve socially desired results. The present model of federal decision making has thrust heavy burdens on business—for product safety, environmental protection, worker safety, etc.—in the name of governmental "economy." He sees this process of converting private enterprises into involuntary agents of government as attenuating the risk-bearing and entrepreneurial characteristics of the business system. Weidenbaum has served as Mallinckrodt Distinguished University Professor at Washington University, St. Louis, since 1969. Combining careers in government and business with academic pursuits, he has served as economist for Boeing Airplane Company and later as Assistant Secretary of the U.S. Treasury Department. He has written extensively on government-business relationships.*

J. Fred Weston *shows that large firms and concentrated industries are generally of benefit to American consumers by enabling them to realize the lower costs and lower prices made possible by economies of scale. His analysis demonstrates that industrial concentration in the U.S. economy has not been increasing, that it is confined to those half-dozen industries also concentrated in other industrialized countries, and that it results from efforts to realize economies of large scale. Concentration has not been enduringly associated with high profits or with price inflation. Hence he concludes that there is no economic foundation for punitive federal legislation or antitrust action against large firms in concentrated industries. Weston has served as Professor of Business Economics and Finance at the University of California, Los Angeles, since 1949. Educated at the University of Chicago, he is one of the nation's most respected scholars in his fields. He has also served as President of the American Finance Association and as President of the Western Economic Association. He is the author of a dozen books and many scientific articles.*

CHANGING MODES OF GOVERNMENT REGULATION OF BUSINESS

John R. Meyer

THE JOINT PUBLIC-PRIVATE MANAGEMENT AGENCY

Early government regulation of industry in the United States was characteristically of the type in which a special agency, usually a creature of Congress, helped manage a particular industry's affairs, often in considerable depth and detail. The Interstate Commerce Commission (ICC), the Federal Communications Commission (FCC), the Federal Power Commission (FPC), the Securities and Exchange Commission (SEC), the Civil Aeronautics Board (CAB), the Nuclear Regulatory Commission (NRC), state public service and public utility commissions—all fitted this basic pattern.

Diverse motives stimulated these early regulatory efforts. Consumer protection was nearly always prominent in the publicly professed motives, and it may even have been dominant in some cases, e.g., the SEC. Development and promotion of a "struggling" infant industry was the major consideration in other instances, e.g., the FCC, AEC, and CAB. Cartelization or stabilization of an industry's markets was still another major incentive. Many scholars believe that this cartelization motive largely explains the ICC's relationship to the railroad industry in the late nineteenth century, and the ready acquiescence of the trucking and inland waterway common carriers to ICC regulation during the 1930s.

The performance of these regulatory agencies in meeting their real or professed objectives has been at least as diverse as their origins and motivations. The general scholarly consensus today is that consumer protection has *not* been a major accomplishment of regulation. Even if an agency starts with emphasis on consumer interests—so the argument goes—the highly individualistic, even personalized, relationship between the agency and the regulated industry is such that, as the industry matures, the temptation to indulge in cartelization becomes overwhelming. Thus, many observers see the CAB as going through a cycle in which it began with promotion and development as its major objective, slid into a more consumer-oriented stance toward the end of the second decade of its existence, and now is drifting into a cartelization-stabilization mode. Similarly, many less skeptical scholars would characterize the ICC as starting with consumer interests paramount, but then accommodating or even promoting cartelization in order to achieve real power in industry affairs.

Neither have the agencies done exceedingly well in protecting *producer* interests, if, indeed, that was their goal. Regulated industries have produced relatively low rates of return on net worth, although common carrier trucking and banking appear to be partial exceptions to the rule. In 1972, three regulated industries ranked near or at the bottom in rate of return: Air Transport at 6.6 percent, Class I Railroads at 3 percent, and Investment Funds at 2.5 percent. These percentages contrast with a 12.1 percent average return for all manufacturing, 12.4 percent for the service industries, and 11.3 percent for trade. Financial difficulties and bankruptcies are rather commonplace in the railroad, airline, and securities industries.

Earnings deficiencies are also suggested by the apparent insufficiency of capital in some regulated industries, notably the electric power industry. In particular, insufficient incentive to invest is alleged in some regulated industries, despite rapidly growing demands for their products. The natural gas industry is cited as the worst recent example of this phenomenon; and many would also claim that electric utilities and telephones constitute apt illustrations of the same problem.

FUNCTIONAL REGULATION

Given this failure to meet either producer or consumer objectives, it is not surprising that alternatives to the joint public-private management format of regulation have arisen. By far the most important alternative has been "functional regulation." Functional regulation started as early as the turn of the century in the form of the antitrust laws. The Federal Trade Commission (FTC), the Robinson-Patman Act, and similar efforts to eliminate "predatory pricing" and other forms of "anticompetitive" behavior also go back many decades. Government's objectives in enacting such legislation are not always clear or consistent. For example, the so-called "fair-trade" laws that permit the fixing of minimum prices represent, in the view of many observers, an attempt to extend the principle of cartelization and thus are anticompetitive in effect.

In general, functional regulation applies to business performance in carrying out a narrow, well-defined business function, in contrast to the application of joint-management regulation to practically all aspects of an enterprise's performance. And functional regulation usually embraces business firms in several industries or throughout the economy.

Examples of functional regulation abound, and the number of instances has grown rapidly within the last decade or so. The most important example, from an economic standpoint, has been the effort to establish an "incomes policy," regulating increases in wages, prices, rents, interest, and dividends. The methods range widely, of course, from "jawboning" to "guideposts" to "freezes" and mandatory controls. The real and psychological impacts can hardly be overestimated. Indeed, economists, public officials, businessmen, and labor leaders are only beginning to sort out their thoughts on the difficult issues involved.

Regulations aimed at environmental improvement are a second economically important category of functional regulation. Environmental controls are not restricted to air and water depollution, but extend to billboards, junkyards, plant location, and so forth. On the whole, the environmental regulations of the last half decade or so constitute an eloquent example of public policy outracing the underlying information or knowledge base. Because complex system interactions or interdependencies are often involved in environmental problems, and the secondary and tertiary effects of a given policy are often not obvious, functional regulations not uncommonly have produced results contradictory to their primary or intended effects.

A third relatively new category of functional regulation has to do with safety both of products and of working conditions. There have been intensified efforts in fields of traditional concern, such as drug certification and coal mining. And regulations have extended into completely new areas, such as automobile design. The development of new technologies, particularly nuclear power, has also led to an increase in government involvement in the safety of employees and of the public.

Attempts to achieve better flows of information to consumers constitute another relatively recent development in functional regulation. Truth-in-lending and unit prices are two important examples. Again, historical roots are relatively deep and long-standing; but only within the last decade has governmental activity become significant. Continued price inflation and the greater involvement of women in politics and business may promote this type of regulation, which could be the "growth sector" of government regulation in the future.

THE PUBLIC-PRIVATE ENTERPRISE

Other important alternatives to either conventional joint-management or functional regulation have emerged in recent years, motivated to some extent by disappointment with previous forms of business regulation. The most important example is certainly the joint public-private enterprise. The Federal National Mortgage Association (Fannie Mae or FNMA), the Communications Satellite Corporation (COMSAT), the U.S. Postal Service, and the proposed Federal National Railway Association (Fannie Rae) exemplify the new species.

The new public-private enterprises have an interesting diversity of origins and motives. Fannie Mae represents a spinoff of a successful government activity that apparently no longer needed the special protection and aid of government to survive, and could benefit from exposure to the competitive pressures of private enterprise. COMSAT embodies a government effort to aid the private sector in developing a new and expensive technology. It contrasts with the joint public-private management agency used to promote new technologies until the late 1940s; indeed, the former AEC may be the last of the "old species." Fannie Rae (assuming it comes into being) would be motivated by failure rather than success: The objective would be to "bail out" the Northeast railroads, a notoriously unsuccessful but economically important sector of the private economy. Fannie Rae would also represent a recognition of an important failure in conventional regulation. Similarly, the Postal Service emerged from failure, though in the public rather than the private sector.

The current fascination with public-private enterprises has led to suggestions to create analogies to the American Telephone and Telegraph Company in other sectors of the economy. For example, a great deal has been said about the adaptability of the "AT&T approach" to the railroad industry; and the question has been debated whether COMSAT should be made more in the image of AT&T. The key questions about the adaptability of the AT&T approach to other industries would appear to be the prevalence of scale economies in these industries and the degree to which they are natural monopolies.

Interest in the public-private enterprise also appears to have been stoked by observation of Japan's postwar economic success. Many would attribute it largely to the unusual degree of cooperation between the government and large private enterprises in Japan. Of course, there were other explanatory factors, such as large pools of under-utilized agricultural labor, a considerable initial gap between world industrial technology and Japan's technology, and very favorable (but unsustainable) terms of trade for manufactured goods as against unprocessed commodities. Also, the adaptability of Japanese methods to other societies remains to be established.

THE PROPENSITY TO DEGRADATION IN REGULATORY AGENCIES

The obvious question is whether the new approaches, functional regulation, and the joint public-private enterprise, will succeed to any greater extent in achieving their professed objectives than the old-style joint-management agencies. The answer is probably *yes* in the short run, and *no* in the long run. A major regularity in previous government efforts to regulate business is the propensity for degradation to occur over time. Late nineteenth-century reports suggest, for example, that the ICC was then a very exciting innovating institution. It represented an important new departure in public policy and attracted some of the best talent of the time. Similarly, there is considerable objective evidence to support an opinion that the SEC has never again been quite as vital as it was in its first few years, when it was under strong and knowledgeable leadership and attracted fine young talent to its staff.

Not all regulatory agencies, of course, follow from the day of their inception an undeviating downward trend in quality and responsiveness. New appointments to many of the regulatory commissions, particularly to the chairman's seat, have often resulted in at least a temporary revival. Nevertheless, most such revivals have been only cyclical fluctuations around a basic downward trend.

If aging is the problem, how does one incorporate change into the regulatory system? One simple legalistic way would be to establish for any new agency an arbitrary cutoff of its life, at say ten years. However, the realities of bureaucratic self-survival, plus the considerable potentiality for a growing community of interests between the agency and the industries being regulated, suggest that any such cutoff date would never be realized. Political inertia would be too large to overcome.

The potentialities for unbiased appraisal of performance that are implicit in the joint public-private enterprise give this approach its special attractiveness. A public-private enterprise, usually being somewhat dependent upon private external financing, would be more exposed to the "corrective audit" that constitutes a fundamental contribution of organized financial markets to a market economy. The extent to which this correction would work in practice, though, is uncertain. Many observers contend that "the audit" really is inoperative, even for completely private enterprises, given the increasingly professional character of managements and the alleged divorce of ownership from control. Moreover, the ultimate corrective in the private sector, the formal takeover by another enterprise, would ordinarily not be available to the joint public-private enterprise. Finally, access to *public* funds could obviously moderate much of the normal financial discipline of capital markets. The experience of other countries with joint enterprises, such as many international "flag" airlines, lends strong confirmatory evidence to these fears. Even with all these limitations, however, the joint public-private enterprise should be somewhat more susceptible to pressures for change than an established government bureaucracy.

The public-private enterprise is mainly a substitute for the joint-management agency. Some forms of regulation, especially those that are functional in character, seem unadaptable to the joint public-private enterprise approach. The usually preferred alternative to formal governmental action to achieve safety, or consumer protection, or any other functional objective, is "self-regulation" by the firms or industries involved. Occasionally, too, spontaneous associations of affected parties such as the Consumers Union and similar organizations may come into being to achieve functional regulatory objectives. On the whole, though, these efforts have probably been less than fully successful. In fact, their failures often induce formal government entry into the field. Nevertheless, in the interests of maintaining options, public policy might consider making grants to support or elicit more private efforts at regulation. A similar line of argument could also justify the tax preferences now given to various forms of cooperative associations.

A central theme in designing future business-government relationships might be the development of even more experimentation and diversity—perhaps to the point of deliberately inducing overlapping jurisdictions between public and private agencies. For example, government agencies, joint public-private corporations, and private enterprises might all compete with each other in providing mail services to the public. Also, change should be institutionalized for government regulatory agencies. A formal cutoff date or a periodic reappraisal of an agency may not work; but it is at least worth a try. The very act of reappraisal should create an opportunity to insert alternative points of view into the record. In a world of limited options, this may be the best that can be done.

THE SOCIAL COSTS OF GOVERNMENTAL INTERVENTION

Roger G. Noll

American governments, at all levels, attempt to manage the operations of many business enterprises and markets. My purpose is to describe the workings of their administrative processes, and to show how they affect the performance of the firms that are subject to them. A major conclusion is that governmental intervention in private markets through the establishment of administrative agencies has, in many instances, exacted an immense cost in reduced economic efficiency of the regulated firms. Four kinds of costs of intervention can be identified; two of them refer to the *diminished incentives* of the regulated firms to perform efficiently, and two refer to the adverse effects of regulation upon *resource allocation* within the managed sectors and the economy as a whole.

FOUR ADVERSE EFFECTS OF GOVERNMENTAL INTERVENTION

The four undesirable effects of governmental intervention on the efficiency of the private sector may conveniently be described as Penncentralization, Lockheedization, Legalization, and Consultantization.

Penncentralization. This is the tendency of the government regulatory process to destroy the incentives of firms to operate efficiently. In the case of the Penn Central Railroad, for example, ICC regulation left little incentive to minimize operating costs under the current technology, or to make timely innovations that would reduce costs or make possible new economically viable services. Regulation has significantly reduced, if not eliminated, the ability of firms to benefit from the gains resulting from improvements in their performance. It has prevented, or significantly retarded, the introduction of economically warranted innovations. It has protected inefficient firms against competition from others more efficient.

Lockheedization. This is the tendency of governmental regulators to subsidize the survival of large, badly managed firms with which they have developed a symbiotic relationship. More than encouraging inefficient, slothful management, this process can create an entirely new industry—the "failure business." When the welfare of a firm comes to depend heavily upon governmental decisions, and when the firm is very large, government officials come to believe that they can no longer afford to permit it to fail. Conversely, corporate management may come to regard government subsidization, directly or indirectly, as a regular, dependable source of revenue. In fact, the financial position of the subsidized firm may be *better* if it periodically fails the test of the private capital market!

Legalization. This is the tendency of the regulatory process to become a labyrinth of procedural complexities that imposes mountainous costs and endless delays on the regulated firms. Formal rules of evidence and procedure cause the administrative process to be expensive to those participating in it. Large resources must be devoted to dealing with the administrators: lawyers, engineers, economists, and managers. The process is long; and the longer it takes to obtain approval for some change in business practices, the less attractive will be the change to the firm. The more complicated the administrative process, the greater the extent to which it is controlled by the legal profession. In the words of Roger C. Cramton, a former chairman of the Administrative Conference of the United States, administrative agencies constitute a "full employment bill for lawyers." Lawyers are trained to be concerned primarily about the maintenance of due process, the protection of private equities, and the ability of a system to achieve consensus. But a process that satisfies the lawyers' conception of fairness is unlikely to be the least expensive method for achieving the same policy outcome.[1]

Consultantization. This is the tendency of the regulatory process to divert scarce creative talent from productive pursuits to redistributive activities. The benefits to a firm from being well-represented before administrative agencies by bright professionals are largely private pecuniary gains. The effect of agency efforts is simply to redistribute wealth among competing claimants, not to increase economic output. Yet the people who participate in the process are among the most intelligent, creative individuals in society. Having them devote their energies to the administrative process reduces their contribution to real economic progress. If complicated administrative procedures were the only available mechanism for achieving redistributions of wealth, these costs might be worthwhile. But such is not the case. The administrative process often becomes far more complex and costly than is necessary to achieve its objectives.

The four inefficiencies arising from the administrative process vary significantly in magnitude among government agencies. To explain their appearance and importance requires an investigation of what might be called the theory of the administrative process—how government officials and participants in private markets interact to produce administrative policies and procedures.

THE TRADITIONAL THEORY
OF THE REGULATORY PROCESS

Let us assume that government agencies seek to maximize "social welfare" or the "public interest." Numerous conceptual models of
bureaucratic behavior are based on this assumption, differing according to their descriptions of how government officials perceive the public interest.[2] Traditional theories in economics, political science, and
sociology, while emphasizing different aspects of the social process, are
quite similar in their basic conceptualization. Although the traditional
view is no longer widely shared, it is a good place to begin because it
provides a benchmark for investigating other theories. Furthermore,
much of modern theory is rooted in the traditional approach.

Traditional sociology, developing from the ideas of Max Weber,
makes few distinctions between public and private organizations. It
views society as requiring the performance of certain "functions" for its
survival. Society creates institutions or "structures" to perform these
functions. Bureaucratic institutions, with formal and impersonal rules
carried out by professionals whose employment is based on objective
measures of competence, represent the most effective mechanism for
performing these essential functions.

Traditional political science, focusing naturally on government institutions, emphasizes the separation of functions among the branches
of the government. Through the workings of the democratic process,
legislation evolving from compromise and bargaining among elected
representatives reflects the public interest. Meanwhile, the development of a career civil service based upon expertise provides objectivity
and freedom from partisanship in the implementation of policies.

Economists view administrative agencies as devices for correcting
inefficiencies arising from various kinds of market imperfections, such
as seller concentration, external effects, and unpredictable fluctuations
in supply and demand. Strangely enough, the *costs of regulation* were
largely ignored by economists until recently, despite their characteristic
concern for economic efficiency. Even the current theoretical literature
in economics on the costs of regulation is traditional in approach.[3] It
assumes that regulatory processes simply limit the profits of a firm that
possesses market power, that the costs of determining and enforcing
the "right" regulatory constraint can be ignored, and that the profit
constraint is applied with sufficient constancy so that its principal effect
on a firm's efficiency is to bias the selection of long-term capital investments. These assumptions are remarkably similar to the assumptions of sociological theories that economists have criticized—that institutions exist to perform every important social function. Both give
scant attention to alternative "functionally equivalent" structures that
might be more cost-effective.

Combining the traditional views of all three disciplines, the following characterization of administrative policy emerges: An "essential function" of a capitalist society is to limit inefficiencies that may arise from the imperfections of markets. One purpose of democratically elected legislatures is to detect serious market imperfections and to establish regulatory agencies to ameliorate them. Because the decisions of these agencies can generate substantial wealth, they are potential targets for corruption. Hence their decision making must be placed in the hands of experts removed from partisan politics. When regulatory policy fails, the causes are one or more of the following: the administrators are poorly selected, being either corrupt or inexpert; the legislative mandate is faulty, either because it lacks clarity or because subsequent events have outdated it; or the agency lacks the authority or the resources to implement its policy effectively.

Unfortunately, empirical studies of regulatory behavior do *not* indicate that this traditional theory, and the policy implications derived from it, have much relevance to the real world. These studies generally support the following characterization of the regulatory process:

First, to the extent that there is a clear majority opinion of the electorate that can be characterized as representing the "public interest," successive delegations of decision making lead to policies that *drift* from this position. A loss of public control occurs through successive delegations—to Congress, to committees and subcommittees of Congress, to the agency, and to lower hierarchical levels in the agency. Furthermore, for a given agency and policy, this drift grows larger through time.

Second, client capture is common. The direction of policy drift away from the majority opinion of the electorate is in the direction of the welfare of the particular groups in closest contact with the administrative agency—namely, the regulated firms.

Third, administrative agencies are inflexible, rigid, and slow to adapt policies to changing external conditions. Decisions tend to be based upon short-run considerations and upon the preservation of the existing structure. This causes agencies to retard technological advancement and to resist new sources of competition, unless they can be shown to leave the existing institutional system largely unchanged.

A POLITICAL-ECONOMIC MODEL
OF THE REGULATORY PROCESS

A model of administrative behavior based upon recent ideas in economics and political science seems more useful than traditional theory in explaining real world conditions. In the political-economic model the relationship between administrators and firms is viewed as complex and dynamic. This theory assumes, as does traditional theory, that administrators try to serve some concept of the public interest. The problem is to identify this public interest in a milieu in which information is uncertain, expensive, and biased; and in a society that contains numerous groups whose interests are conflicting rather than harmonious.

The political-economic theory focuses on the external signals received by an agency regarding its performance. Agencies perform in "theatres of external judgment"—i.e., institutional environments in which external entities are able to influence their policies and pass judgment on their performances. Among these are the courts, to whom those disgruntled with an agency decision can appeal; congressional subcommittees that oversee the agency's program and budget; the examiners of the federal Office of Management and Budget; and the press, whose primary concern is the managed industry.

From each theatre of external judgment the agency receives a flow of performance indicators, expressing approval or disapproval with its decisions. An agency will view the public interest as having been served by a decision if these indicators show approval. If the feedback is positive, if its budget requests and legislative proposals are generally well-received by the overseeing congressional subcommittees, if its encounters with congressmen are free of serious conflict, if agency decisions are rarely appealed to the courts, if the courts normally uphold the agency's decisions upon appeal, and if the managed market's performance is sufficiently high that journalistic inquiries into the agency's policies are rarely made, then the agency will conclude that it is serving the public interest well.

REGULATORY BIAS IN FAVOR OF
REPRESENTED INTERESTS

This system leads to a systematic bias in decisions, because of unevenness of representation of interests in the decision making process. Because participation in the regulatory process is expensive, the effectiveness with which a group can protect its equities depends upon the resources it has available. Not all private interests of equal size will have equal representation. Generally, the smaller the group, the higher the per capita stake of each member in the issue, the more dependent will be the success of the group on the participation of each member, and the greater the likelihood that the group will become organized to represent its interests.

A group that has become organized to represent itself before a regulatory agency is a potential threat. It may appeal the agency's decision to the courts, lobby congressmen about the error of the agency's ways, or wage a public campaign in support of policies contrary to those established by the agency. Hence, an agency attempting to avoid negative feedback will develop complicated decision-making procedures for several reasons. First, they will enable the agency to gauge the interests of the represented groups in the issue at hand, and thereby better estimate the probability that each will appeal any particular decision. Second, they will make participation in the process more expensive, thereby reducing the number of groups entering the process and the number of potential threats to appeal. Third, they will give outsiders the impression that the agency has behaved fairly in gathering information and listening to divergent points of view, thereby enhancing the chance that the agency will win any appeal to the courts or to Congress.

Regulators devote most of their attention to the effects of their policies on *well-represented* special interest groups. As a natural consequence of the adversary system, the information flowing to the agency will be systematically biased against unrepresented groups. To minimize the chance of being rebuffed by the courts or the legislature, the agency will be inclined to make decisions that favor represented groups. If more than one group is well-represented on a particular issue, the agency will first hold excruciatingly long proceedings to gather information before making a decision. This makes participation in the process even more costly, so that some groups will drop out. Also, it postpones the day when an appeal must be fought. When a decision is finally made, the agency will seek a compromise between the well-represented groups. By giving them all a stake in the decision, the incentive to appeal is reduced.

REGULATORY BIAS AGAINST INNOVATION

This behavior can be especially costly when agencies are faced with a decision on whether to permit the regulated industry to adopt a new technology. Because innovation tends to redistribute wealth among participants in private markets, the possibility of a major innovation will cause groups with stakes in *current* technology to be well-represented in the proceedings. The reluctance of the administrator to permit the innovation arises from the uncertainty inherent in change. A new method may be expected to produce great benefits, but usually there is some chance that it can cause a deterioration in service to the public. The agency thus faces an asymmetric penalty for mistakes.

Preventing a technology that would have been worthwhile may generate criticism; but it will be based on conjectural information about the potential of the new technology. And those who would have benefited from the new technology probably will not be a source of criticism because many will not be aware of the size of their potential gains. On the other hand, *adopting* a technology that is not successful causes the agency to share in the blame for service failure; and it is bound to be criticized by those who lost business because of the new technology.

We see an inherent dilemma in the regulatory process. For innovations *favored* by present producers, an agency will be most likely to approve a timely adoption if the producers are represented and if the producers' principal threat to the agency is an appeal to Congress and to the public rather than to the courts. But this type of regulatory environment will not be favorable for innovations that present producers perceive as *opposed* to their interests, such as improved products, more worker safety, reduced environmental damage, or reduced costs. However, the latter types of innovations will receive more favorable treatment by the agency if those who would benefit by them are represented in the proceedings. When a regulatory agency becomes the adjudicator of conflicts among represented groups who, among other things, threaten court appeals of agency decisions, a retarded rate of adoption of innovations of the first type results. While more diverse representation makes an agency more likely to exercise effective control over producers, by the same token it may increase the delay and the costs of adopting economically warranted technological change.

ALTERNATIVE ESCAPES
FROM REGULATORY DILEMMAS

The potential escapes from the dilemmas of regulation require fundamental changes in the regulatory environment. One approach is to *merge* the opposing interests in order to reduce the number of conflicts an agency must settle. The rationale for the "single entity" proposal in international communications was that, only by merging the international carriers, would the FCC and the industry make a rational choice among technologies (cables versus satellites). Of course, such mergers improve the ability of producers to represent themselves effectively, thereby reducing the control of the administrative agency over the managed market.

Another approach is to replace institutionalized protection of private interests with *direct compensation*. The disappearance of CAB's subsidy of domestic airlines did not result in the bankruptcy of inefficient carriers or the abandonment of subsidized routes. Instead, the direct subsidies were replaced by price regulations to protect high-cost firms and to create cross-subsidization—the transfer of excess profits on some routes to offset losses on other routes of the same firm. Many studies show that direct compensation is far cheaper than institutionalized protection. It would, in several instances, have led to more rapid adoption of new technologies that were retarded because of their adverse effect on vested interests. Piggyback truck-rail shipping, cable television, and deferred automobile emission standards are all cases in point. Of course, even direct compensation is not without costs. It requires a complicated procedure for determining equity losses, and it blunts incentives for efficiency and innovativeness (if competition proves too tough, compensation awaits).

A third approach is to break away from the model of regulation by expert judgment, and to have, for example, a *direct election of regulatory authorities* or referenda on administrative policies. In some states, public utility commissions are directly elected rather than appointed, but no assessment has been made of the effects on their behavior. An important study by Charles R. Plott on local urban renewal authorities, however, does show that a requirement that urban renewal plans substantially pass a referendum reduces the extent to which an urban renewal authority designs projects to suit special interests.[4] But an election-referendum approach does raise problems of its own. Given the great extent of regulation, it would lead to a horrendously complicated ballot. Such "bedsheet ballots" require considerable voter sophistication if the results are to be valid indicators of preferences.

The "external signal" theory of administrative behavior has one additional important implication. Some issues motivate political action because they have achieved "salience," that is, importance to sufficiently large blocs of voters to become important in elections. For example, inflation, environmental protection, and energy shortages have influenced the character of regulatory decisions in the past few years because of their overriding political importance, transcending particularized group lobbying efforts. Certainly a blow would be struck for giving salient issues more weight in the regulatory decision-making process if more stringent controls were imposed on the financing of political campaigns. This would reduce the indirect influence of well-organized special interest groups over regulatory agencies via friendly congressmen, thereby making the agencies more sensitive to the will of the general electorate.

NOTES

1. This is not to argue that lawyers are indifferent to the procedural costs of decision making, although there may be an element of this. Where an economist perceives a procedural cost a lawyer sees income. But even if lawyers who run administrative agencies attempt to achieve given degrees of institutionalized protection of private equities and of procedural niceties for minimum feasible cost, the performance of the managed market will still fail a test of economic efficiency.

2. The paradox established by the Kaldor-Hicks-Scitovsky controversy over compensation principles and the literature on social choice theory, beginning with Arrow's possibility theorem, cast grave doubts on the existence of a well-defined, consistent "public interest." But this does not imply any fundamental error in public-interest theories of bureaucratic behavior. As long as officials *believe* that a public interest has been defined for them and act to serve it, the fact that the public interest they perceive lacks interesting normative properties is inessential to the positive theory of their behavior.

3. This refers to the so-called A-J effect on the efficiency of resource utilization that arises when rate-of-return regulation is imposed on a profit-seeking enterprise. See Harvey Averch and Leland L. Johnson, "The Behavior of the Firm under Regulatory Constraint," *American Economic Review* 52(1962): 1053–69; and William J. Baumol and Alvin Klevorick, "Imput Choices and Rate-of-Return Regulation: An Overview of the Discussion," *Bell Journal* 1 (1970): 162–90.

4. Charles R. Plott, "Some Organizational Influences on Urban Renewal Decisions," *American Economic Review, Papers and Proceedings* 58 (1968): 306–21.

A NEW MODEL OF
GOVERNMENTAL DECISION MAKING

Murray L. Weidenbaum

ADVERSARY OR PEACEFUL COEXISTER

The relationships between business and government in the United States can be described as being basically adversary in nature. The government probes, inspects, taxes, influences, regulates, and punishes business. At least that appears to be the dominant view in the business world and in many quarters of the public sector. And in many ways it appears to come uncomfortably close to reality. Certainly, the vast majority of public policy changes in recent years have been in that direction. Environmental controls, job safety inspections, equal employment opportunity enforcement, consumer product safety regulations, and the obligation of business to report items varying from the illnesses of employees to foreign currency transactions—all illustrate the trend.

The contrast is striking between the American relationship and what is often taken to be the dominant European and Japanese approach—a "partnership" or, at least, close cooperation between business and government. This has led to suggestions that we should import the foreign model, in order to improve our competitive position abroad as well as to enhance productivity at home. But the submergence of the public, and especially the consumer, interest that might result from such a merger of big government and big business would be a cause of great concern.

Yet the status quo seems undesirable. It does not seem sensible to expect American business to be successful in waging a two-front war, struggling against increasing governmental encroachment at home, while competing against government-supported enterprises abroad. Hence a third approach should be considered, a variant of that attitude toward international relations called "peaceful coexistence." We should explore the possibilities of a sensible division of labor between the public and private sectors in achieving basic national objectives. In order to explain the implications of this concept, let us briefly describe the current method of setting national priorities that impact upon business. Then, we present a new model of decision making based upon a more productive business-government relationship.

THE PRESENT NATIONAL
PRIORITY-SETTING PROCESS

In practice, decisions on government budgets, particularly on the spending side, have been made "in the small." Congress has acted on many individual authorization bills and appropriation statutes. The bits and pieces were then added up on a functional basis—so much for defense, so much for welfare, so much for education, and so on. In this approach, business—if it is thought about at all—is regarded as an input, a tool or mechanism for achieving a governmental purpose. In defense spending, business firms are very heavily utilized; in the rapidly expanding income-maintenance programs, they are hardly involved at all. Thus, the shift in budget priorities in recent years from warfare to welfare, has meant—perhaps unwittingly—a reduced emphasis on the employment of business in carrying out national purposes. The earlier concern about moving toward a "contract state," in which key government responsibilities are delegated to private corporations, has faded away.

Another fiscal development has been occurring which raises quite different concerns. The desire to exercise more control over the growth of the federal budget—be that due to concern over the inflationary effects of budget deficits or to a philosophical resistance to the growth of the public sector—has led to an effort to "economize" on direct government spending. Increasingly, the federal government has been relying on mechanisms designed to help accomplish a given national objective without spending more public money for the purpose. The newer approach is to influence private outlays to achieve the same ends. Thus, rather than make the public treasury bear the full burden of cleaning up environmental pollution, private firms are required to devote more resources to that purpose. Rather than have the federal government provide funds directly to individuals and institutions that apparently cannot obtain private financing, public guarantees, or subsidies are offered to induce private lenders to meet these needs. The resistance to socialized medicine has led to a variety of recent proposals to require employers to pay a share of the cost of health insurance for their employees and their families. Although neither federal operation nor financing of health care would be required, an increased financial burden would be placed on business, with the side-effect of making labor more costly and somewhat less attractive vis-à-vis capital investment. These fiscal "shortcuts," it should be understood, are not part of any conscious new policy to increase governmental influence over the private sector. But they have that effect.

Virtually every major department of the typical U.S. industrial corporation has one or more federal agencies that control or strongly influence its internal decision making. For example, the company's production department is now aware of the presence of the U.S. Labor Department's occupational safety and health (OSHA) inspector. The firm's marketing department must take account of the embryonic Consumer Product Safety Commission. Its personnel department must avoid running afoul of equal employment opportunity regulations as well as wage and hour requirements. The finance department must keep its books and make its financial reports to satisfy the IRS and the SEC, and possibly government-sponsored credit agencies as well. The research and development department must work on products and processes that meet the requirements of the EPA.

Of course, only a Scrooge would quarrel with the desirability of safer working conditions, better products for the consumer, eliminating discrimination in employment, and reducing environmental pollution. Nevertheless, the costs vis-à-vis the benefits that result from following this course of national policy have never been explicitly examined and weighed against each other. The costs our society pays for using this route of "economizing" on direct government expenditures are much more than the sum of the unproductive reporting, monitoring, and other overhead expenses incurred in both the public and the private sectors—and these are substantial. *The hidden high price that we pay is the attenuation of the risk-bearing and entrepreneurial characteristics of our private enterprise system,* which in the past have contributed mightily to rapid rates of innovation, productivity, and growth.

The future consequences of pursuing the path on which we have embarked can be seen by examining the military hardware industry—a sector of American industry that already has gone far down the road of reliance upon governmental leadership and assistance. What we see is most disconcerting. Over a period of three decades, the major defense contractors have grown accustomed to federal government decisions on which products are to be produced, how the firm is to produce them, how fixed and working capital are to be provided; and in the process the government often assumes a major portion of the risk. More Lockheeds and General Dynamicses—or more C5As and TFXs (to cite two well-known products of the two most government-dependent large defense contractors)—would hardly be a way of achieving either greater domestic productivity or greater international competitiveness.

A NEW MODEL FOR SETTING NATIONAL PRIORITIES

Clearly, we need to arrest the tendency for government to involve itself increasingly in what essentially is internal business decision making. The model that we should follow is to determine national priorities by a two-step process. The first step should be to determine how much of our resources should be devoted to defense, health, welfare, education, and other functions. The second should be to allocate responsibilities for each function between the public and private sectors of the economy. This type of indicative planning would recognize that governmental nibbling away at business prerogatives and entrepreneurial characteristics has a very substantial cost—a reduced effectiveness in achieving some basic national objectives. This proposed planning process would also take account of the different mix of constituencies that the public and private sectors are primarily geared to serve.

In this day when benefit-cost analysis has become fashionable, we should not be oblivious to the very real, if not easily measured, effects of converting private organizations into involuntary agents of the federal establishment. Rather than pursuing the current course, the nation should determine which of its objectives can be achieved more effectively in the private sector. Then it should create an environment that is conducive to the attainment of those objectives by business. It would appear reasonable to expect that primarily *social* objectives—such as improved police services—would mainly be the province of government. And primarily *economic* objectives—notably training, motivating, and employing the bulk of the nation's work force—would be viewed mainly as a responsibility of the private sector.

The new model of national decision making envisioned here does not call for an abdication of government concern with the substantive issues. Rather, it would require a redirection of the methods of achieving worthy ends. In the environmental area, for example, tax incentives should replace much of the current dependence on direct controls. Imaginative use of "sumptuary" excise taxation—to which we have grown accustomed in the cases of tobacco products and alcoholic beverages—can be used to alter basic production and consumption patterns. The desired results would no longer be accomplished by fiat, but by making the high-pollutant product or service more expensive relative to the low-pollutant product or service. The guiding principle would be that people and institutions pollute because it is easier, cheaper, or more profitable to do so, and not because they enjoy messing up the environment. In lieu of a corps of inspectors or regulators, we would use the price system to make polluting harder, more expensive, and less profitable.

There is a parallel here to the operation of a tariff system. Even a low tariff instituted ostensibly only for revenue purposes usually keeps out some products. The higher the rate, the closer it comes to becoming a "protective" tariff to the point of keeping out the undesired item entirely. The growing scarcity of energy sources provides another opportunity for choosing between greater government control of industry (allocations and rationing) and use of markets to achieve the same results, by imposing heavier taxes on the use of energy and thereby reducing the demand for it. The market approach is hardly likely to gain the enthusiastic support of the energy industry; yet it would strengthen the business system by obviating the need for direct governmental controls. The tax increase, in effect, would be in lieu of a price increase. Moreover, the results could be more equitable, to the extent that a portion of the proceeds are used, *via* cash rebates, to soften the adverse impacts on the low-income population.

MARKET VERSUS BUREAUCRATIC
REGULATION OF BUSINESS

Other areas of the economy could benefit from using alternatives to government intervention in business operations. One area of intervention that has expanded substantially in recent years concerns the flow of saving and investment, which is a very basic aspect of a capitalistic economy. As a result of the expanded use of government-sponsored credit agencies, such as Fanny Mae or the Federal Land Banks, a rising portion—a third or more in recent years—of all the funds raised in private capital markets now funnel through these federal financial intermediaries. In every period of credit tightness, there is a clamor to set up additional agencies, such as an Aerospace Reconstruction Finance Corporation or an Energy Research and Development Corporation, to assure yet another category of borrowers ready access to credit.

Yet none of these federal instrumentalities *add* to the available pool of investment funds. In practice, their operations literally amount to robbing Peter to pay Paul. They reduce the ability of the market to allocate funds to the more efficient undertakings. A positive and fruitful approach to national policy in this area would be to create an economic environment that provides more incentive to individuals and business firms to save, and thus generates more investment funds for the use of society as a whole.

In dealing with occupational safety and health (OSHA)—a sore point in the business-government relationship—government appears to have lost sight of the basic objective—a safer working environment. The current emphasis is on the punishment of violations, whether or not they are intentional. (Business firms actually have been discouraged from seeking federal assistance for their efforts at voluntary compliance!) A positive approach by government would focus efforts on reduction of the accident and health hazards in an industry, rather than on the prescription of specific practices to be followed by a company. This would leave open to the management of a company the choice of equipment, working rules, employee training, and other variables needed to achieve the results prescribed by law. Experience suggests that the best mix of methods, entailing the least loss of productivity, will vary from plant to plant, from firm to firm, and over time.

The results of such decentralized decision making will not necessarily coincide with those of a more centralized system. We may have a different mix of goods and services. But if our nation's resources are utilized more effectively as a result of reducing the burden of government controls, the overall national output would increase. Economic welfare would be enhanced.

The new division of labor between the public and private sectors envisioned here should not be expected to remain invariant over time. It should change with underlying circumstances—foreign and domestic—and as experience is gained from following a strategy of peaceful coexistence between business and government. The dividing line between public and private responsibilities probably will shift back and forth in the future, rather than move in a single direction.

BIG FIRMS, CONCENTRATED INDUSTRIES, AND ANTITRUST POLICIES

J. Fred Weston

THE RESURGENCE OF INTEREST IN BIG BUSINESS

The large business corporation is the lightning rod that attracts public criticism of the American business system. Its operations are typically widespread and highly visible. The large firm is generally believed (although proof is lacking) to possess great economic and political power. As the most visible institution of the capitalist economy, it is naturally blamed by the public for the shortcomings in economic performance, and the disappointments in popular expectations of rising standards of living.

With the growth of public interest in the social responsibilities of business, the large firm has been viewed even more critically in recent years.[1] Big companies have been much criticized for contributing to environmental pollution, because much heavy manufacturing activity is carried on by large firms in such concentrated industries as steel, chemicals, nonferrous metals, and motor vehicles. Some economists have also charged that large firms have been especially guilty of discrimination in employment.[2] Although many of these allegations cannot stand the test of factual evidence, most observers would agree that big corporations should exhibit leadership in this field.

The conglomerate movement of the 1960s again raised the issues of macroeconomic concentration, mergers of large companies, and the relation between the size of the firm and its economic and political power. Issues of corporate bigness and industrial concentration have also acquired a global dimension in recent years, as a result of the postwar spread of multinational corporations and the new competition in each country from foreign-based firms. All of these factors account for the increased attention to the role of large corporations in the economy and their political, economic, and social effects. It is timely to review the findings of recent economic research on this subject, with the aim of finding valid guides to public policies toward big business, and toward the concentrated industries wherein they are most frequently found.

RECENT PUBLIC POLICIES IN INDUSTRIAL ORGANIZATION

Historically, the earliest and most important public policies to regulate the organization of U.S. industry and the role of big firms, were the antimonopoly laws of the states. Antitrust enforcement really began, however, with the passage of the Sherman Act by Congress in 1890, which put the much greater political power of the federal government behind efforts to maintain competition.

The Celler-Kefauver Act of 1950 represented an important milestone in the evolution of antitrust legislation. It closed a loophole in the earlier Clayton Act by making illegal the acquisition of the assets of companies as well as acquisition of their equity securities. Celler-Kefauver also tightened the constraints against business mergers, by making a merger illegal if there was a *trend* toward concentration in an industry, thereby creating a presumption of incipient tendencies toward monopoly. It delineated markets more narrowly by defining them as "a line of commerce" in any section of the nation. With narrower markets, the market shares of large firms automatically increased, and industries showed higher levels of concentration. It has been said that Celler-Kefauver virtually stopped horizontal and vertical mergers between large companies; indeed, the evidence shows that the predominant and increasing proportion of mergers during the 1960s were of the conglomerate type (Table 1).

TABLE 1

Large Merger Activity, 1960–70
(Percent of Total Large Mergers)*

			Type of Merger		
	HORIZONTAL	VERTICAL	CONGLOMERATE		
Year			Unrelated or "Pure" Conglomerate**	Product or Market Extension	Total
1960	15.6	15.6	12.5	56.2	68.8
1961	18.3	21.7	18.3	41.7	60.0
1962	13.8	18.8	18.8	48.8	67.5
1963	14.6	15.9	17.1	52.4	69.5
1964	19.8	15.4	7.7	57.1	64.8
1965	16.5	13.2	19.8	50.5	70.3
1966	10.9	10.9	22.8	55.4	78.2
1967	6.5	9.5	23.8	60.1	83.9
1968	6.3	9.2	25.1	59.4	84.5
1969	9.0	9.7	33.5	47.7	81.3
1970	9.2	3.1	38.8	49.0	87.8

* Large mergers are defined to include firms with total assets of $10 million or more.

**Unrelated or "pure" conglomerate refers to those mergers in which there is no discernible product relationship between the merging parties.

Source: Bureau of Economics, Federal Trade Commission.

Conglomerate merger activity mounted through the early 1960s and rose to a feverish pace during the second half of the decade. After the severe setback in common stock prices during 1968, however, the movement receded sharply, a resettling process took place, and conglomerates were assessed more soberly. Changes in the tax laws, discouraging the use of debt in acquisitions, as well as threats of legal action, helped to discourage conglomeration. Moreover, the experience of conglomerate firms showed that diversification by external acquisition was more difficult to manage than diversification developed internally. Finally, it appears likely that the hectic merger activity of the late 1960s reduced the supply of synergistic opportunities. Recent conglomerate activity has been in the direction of divestiture.

During the past several years, congressional attention has turned to the concentrated industries, which have been criticized on many grounds. In this atmosphere of criticism the logic of the Celler-Kefauver Act was extended: If the law prohibits concentration by merger, why should it leave *existing* concentration untouched, particularly when it is argued that in many industries the existing concentration resulted from mergers. Hence, recurrent proposals have been made for "deconcentration" of concentrated industries.

Most prominent of these proposals is the Industrial Reorganization Bill of 1973 proposed by Senator Hart of Michigan. This bill sets forth three tests of monopoly power. If a firm fails on any *one* of the three, it would carry the burden of proof that it was not a monopolist before the Industrial Reorganization Commission, proposed to have powers similar to those of the FTC. The first test is whether the four-firm concentration ratio exceeds 50 percent. The second test is whether the after-tax rate of return on equity exceeds 15 percent for five or more successive years. The third test is whether price competition exists in the industry.

The Hart Bill has been presented by its author as only a mild extension of the Sherman Act, in that it removes the apparent historical precedent of a requirement to show "intent to monopolize." In the judgment of many others, however, the Hart Bill goes far beyond this. It has a good chance of passage.

Illustrative of the influence of Senator Hart was his ability to have attached to the Alaskan Pipeline Bill an amendment that transfers authority for approval of the FTC's Line of Business Reporting Program from the Office of Management and Budget (OMB) to the General Accounting Office (GAO). The Line of Business Reporting Program may be regarded as the other half of what is proposed by the Hart Bill, in that it represents the implementation aspects of deconcentration. It requires that every firm (initially in a selected list of 350), shall submit an income statement and balance sheet in considerable detail for each "line of business" that accounts for $10 million or more in annual sales.

A new industrial classification scheme is proposed for defining "lines of business," which focuses in considerable detail on the most concentrated of the traditional 4-digit standard industrial classification industries used by the Bureau of the Census. Manifestly, if a firm can and does separate any segment of its activity for financial reporting, legally required divestiture is thereby facilitated.

THE STRUCTURAL THEORY OF ANTITRUST

The structural theory of antitrust holds that, when the concentration of an industry (the proportion of business done by the top four or top eight firms) exceeds a specified percentage, the effects on competition will be adverse [1, 7, 22]. Thus the Hart Bill asserts that, when the share of the largest four firms of an industry exceeds 50 percent of industry sales, there is presumptive evidence of the existence of monopoly power. Earlier empirical research yielded results that appeared to be consistent with this theoretical model [30, 31, 35]. The structural theory was embraced by the U.S. Supreme Court in a stream of decisions running from the *Philadelphia Bank* case (1963) through *Von's Shopping Bag* (1966). In most of these cases, little defense was made to the assumption of the structural theory that concentration, per se, is anticompetitive. Instead, defenses primarily concerned the definition of the market, and attempted to prove that in an appropriately broad market concentration was not high. The acme of the structural approach was reached in the merger guidelines of the Department of Justice announced on May 30, 1968; and also in the FTC's 1972 complaint in the *Cereal* case that oligopoly can be *equated* to "shared monopoly."

But as the structural theory has moved to a pinnacle of dominance in public policy, defects in the doctrine have become increasingly evident. Recent empirical research into the relations between concentration and business behavior is showing that the structural theory requires reassessment. The field of industrial economics is, therefore, in considerable ferment. Many recent writings vigorously question both the theory and the empirical evidence for structuralism. The central issues in dispute are: (1) the extent of concentration, (2) the causes of concentration, (3) the relation of concentration to profits, and (4) the relation of concentration to prices. We examine these subjects briefly in turn.

The Extent and Trends of
Industrial Concentration

Concentration can be viewed from a *macro* standpoint or from a *micro* standpoint. The alarms that have sounded in connection with the alleged rising tide of concentration have been expressed mainly in connection with macroconcentration—the share of the national income produced by the 200 largest industrial corporations. (*Macro* may also refer to the share of the economy comprised by the 50, 100, or 200 largest manufacturing or industrial corporations. *Industrial* is generally understood to include manufacturing and mining, of which mining contributes only a small portion.)

Most of the debate on concentration relates to manufacturing firms, although manufacturing now accounts for less than one third of the economy, while wholesale and retail trade plus services now constitute a segment of the economy slightly larger than manufacturing (Table 2). In 1970, for example, total national income was $800 billion, of which 27.5 percent was accounted for by manufacturing.

TABLE 2
U.S. National Income by Industrial Division, 1970

Industrial Division	Amount (In Billions of Dollars)	Percent of Total
Agriculture, forestry, and fisheries	24.6	3.1
Mining and construction	49.6	6.2
Manufacturing	220.4	27.5
Transportation	30.3	3.9
Communications	16.3	2.0
Electric, gas, and sanitary services	14.7	1.8
Wholesale and retail trade	121.7	15.2
Finance, insurance, and real estate	88.3	11.0
Services	104.4	13.0
Government and government enterprises	125.2	15.6
Other	4.6	.6
Total, all industries	$800.1	100.0

Source: *Survey of Current Business*, vol. 51, May 1971, table 7, p. 12, U.S. Department of Commerce, Office of Business Economics.

What are the facts about concentration? Is it increasing? Is it dangerous to our economic or social health? The 200 largest industrial corporations in 1968 held 48.6 percent of all manufacturing assets in 1954 and 62.3 percent by 1968. This represents an increase of roughly 1 percentage point per year (Table 3). By extrapolating this trend, it would appear that 40 years after 1968 the 200 largest industrial corporations will account for more than 100 percent of all manufacturing assets! But what is relevant is the power of the 200 largest firms *in 1954* to grow. In 1954 these firms held 50.8 percent of total manufacturing assets, and 14 years later they held 51.2 percent—a gain of 0.4 percent, which is statistically insignificant. In other words, the 200 largest firms at the earlier date simply maintained their share of all manufacturing assets, while the collective share of other firms became larger. Also, the

TABLE 3

**Trends in Share of the 200 Largest U.S. Industrial Corporations, 1954–68
(Total Assets in Billions of Dollars)**

GROUP OF CORPORATIONS	1954		1968		PERCENTAGE CHANGE
	Amount	Percent	Amount	Percent	
200 Largest in 1954	$ 91	50.8	$249	51.2	.4
200 Largest in 1968	87	48.6	303	62.3	13.7
200 Largest in 1954 and in 1968	91	50.8	303	62.3	11.5
Total, all manufacturing corporations	179	100.0	486	100.0	

Source: Betty Bock, *Statistical Games and the "200 Largest" Industrials: 1954 and 1968,* Studies in Business Economics, no. 115 (New York: The Conference Board, 1970), table 1, p. 10.

period 1954-68 is unusual in that much conglomerate merger activity took place; and the extent to which many of these conglomerates will hold together in the future remains to be seen.

Finally, we should observe that, when the position of the largest firms is measured by their share of *value added* by manufacture —which measures their position in real economic activity—the share of the 200 largest firms in 1967 was only 42 percent, although they owned 68 percent of total manufacturing assets [cf. 22]. And the increase in macroconcentration since 1954 is negligible when measured by value added. Evidently, the belief in a strong trend toward macroconcentration in the U.S. economy lacks a factual foundation (Table 4).

TABLE 4

Share of Value Added by Manufacture, 1947–67

Year	All Manufacturing Companies (In Millions of Dollars)	PERCENT OF VALUE ADDED IN EACH YEAR			PERCENT CHANGE IN VALUE ADDED DURING EACH PERIOD		
		200 Largest	100 Largest	50 Largest	200 Largest	100 Largest	50 Largest
1947	$ 74.290	30	23	17			
1954	117.032	37	30	23	7	7	6
1958	141.541	38	30	23	1	0	0
1963	192.103	41	33	25	3	3	2
1967	262.131	42	33	25	1	0	0

Source: J. Fred Weston and Stanley I. Ornstein, *The Impact of Large Firms on the U.S. Economy* (Lexington, Mass.: D.C. Heath, 1973), p. 6.

Trends in microconcentration, or concentration of firms in specified industries, have been the subject of a number of studies. The simplest valid statement that can be made is that there has not been much change in microconcentration in recent years nor, indeed, since 1900. If one begins his study in the Great Depression of the 1930s, he can prove that industrial concentration has decreased, because concentration tends to be relatively high in a period of depression. If one begins his study right after World War II, when small firms boomed in a time of pervasive shortages, he can show that concentration increased thereafter. The truth is that, while shifts have taken place in the economy, *there is no apparent major trend in U.S. industrial concentration.*

TABLE 5

Distribution of Manufacturing Industries, 1966

Percentage of Concentration Ratios	VALUE OF SHIPMENTS		MANUFACTURING INDUSTRIES	
	Amount (In Billions) of Dollars)	Percent of Total	Number	Percent of Total
Over 75	$ 66	14	33	9
50–74	89	19	90	24
25–49	189	40	154	40
Less than 25	124	27	105	27
Total	$468	100	382	100

Source: Weston and Ornstein, *The Impact of Large Firms,* p. 9.

Table 5 shows how the number and value of shipments of U.S. manufacturing industries were distributed among the quartiles of four-firm concentration ratios during 1966. This distribution has been fairly constant over the years.

The Causes of Concentration

One way to assess the structural theory that equates high concentration with "shared monopoly" is to analyze the causes of industrial concentration. Does concentration result from fundamental forces producing economic benefits, or does it reflect distortions of normal economic processes, such as a search by a big corporation for market power?

In his book, *International Differences in Industrial Structure,* Professor Bain [6] presents data which show that for the *same* industries, concentration ratios are generally higher in Western foreign countries than in the United States; that the industries in which foreign concentration is high are generally the same as those in which U.S. concentration is high; and that the industries that are *not* concentrated in foreign countries are generally the same as the unconcentrated industries in this country [cf. 27]. These data strongly suggest that fundamental technological and economic factors determine the degree of concentration of industries in all market economies.

Moreover, a study of communist economies by Lars Engwall [18], including the USSR, found that industrial concentration was *higher* than in the United States.[3] Centralized planning can, of course, be combined with decentralized production to any degree that efficiency dictates. The higher degree of concentration he observed in centrally-planned economies is further evidence that large-scale operations and the accompanying concentration do yield economies of scale.

Another cause of industrial concentration is the advancing technology of management of business firms. Respondents to Professor Bain's survey of the early 1950s were unable to explain the nature of managerial economies of scale or of multiplant economies [5]. But the sources of managerial and multiproduct, multiplant returns to scale have since been identified [36, 41, 43, 44]. A basis is now provided for repeating Bain's study, using these new theoretical concepts as a guide.[4] There is positive evidence that continuity of management organization is an important factor in the efficiency of large firms [41]. This suggests that there would be important losses in managerial efficiencies if these firms were broken up.

In summary, recent evidence suggests that differences in concentration among industries are explained by underlying forces, the most important of which are economies of scale.

The Relation Between
Concentration and Profit
If high concentration is due primarily to technological and economic forces, how has it affected the performance of firms in the resulting oligopolistic industries? Much of the older economic research on performance has proceeded within the narrow confines of the atomistic market model upon which the structural theory is based. It has been preoccupied with profits, viewed as a putative indicator of monopoly power. The possibility that relatively high profits might result from superior efficiency was ignored. In Bain's 1951 article [3] he suggested the critical level of eight-firm concentration was 70 percent. He found that industries with concentrations of 70 percent or more had higher average profit rates than the less-concentrated industries.

(His data, however, also included unconcentrated industries that had relatively high average profits.) Bain presented his results with many qualifications. A number of subsequent studies appeared to support his findings, and great importance came to be attached to these results. It was argued that, if high concentration is associated with high profits, this is evidence of collusion or monopoly power in concentrated industries.

In recent years, however, new studies have substantially altered our knowledge of the relations between concentration and profit rates. Yale Brozen has examined various aspects of the original Bain thesis. He found that industries with the highest profit rates at the time of Bain's study *subsequently* expanded at a relatively high rate, and their profits then trended downward toward the average of all manufacturing industries. Conversely, firms in those industries with low profit rates in an earlier period subsequently expanded at a lower rate and their profits trended upward toward the average for all manufacturing industries [12, 13]. This is very powerful evidence that competitive processes were, in fact, operating. Clearly, public policy need not be concerned with temporary monopoly power that is being steadily eroded by competition.

Indeed, when Brozen expanded Bain's original list by including some additional firms from each industry, *no* relation was found between concentration and profits. Other recent studies reinforce Brozen's findings. Professor Ornstein [23] applied a multiple regression analysis to the investigation of concentration and profits. He found that profit rates are statistically related to economies of scale in production and to growth rates of both the industry and firms, but *not* to concentration. The logic of his study is that no link has been established between the structural theory and profitability. Factors other than concentration could explain the association between concentration and profit that had been observed in simple correlation studies.

The Relation of Concentration to Prices

Our unfortunate experience with inflation since 1965 has highlighted the relation between industrial concentration and prices. Many statements refer to large firms as a primary cause of inflation. But the evidence is to the contrary. The fact is that *there is an inverse relation between the degree of concentration and the extent of price increases:* The more concentrated the industry, the smaller the price increase; and vice versa. Indeed, between 1958 and 1966, there were three periods during which, on the average, prices of the most concentrated industries (those in the "over 75%" quartile) fell, while prices in the less concentrated industries rose (Table 6).

TABLE 6

Average Annual Percentage Price Change by Level of Industry Concentration for Selected Time Periods, 1954–73

PERIOD	CRQ LESS THAN 25%	CRQ 25–49%	CRQ 50–74%	CRQ OVER 75%	ALL
Number of Observations	132	150	76	23	381
1954–58	1.70 (.23)	1.79 (.22)	1.77 (.29)	1.58 (.67)	1.74 (.14)
Number of Observations	65	89	59	22	235
1958–63	0.28 (.20)	0.40 (.16)	0.39 (.29)	–0.24 (.42)	0.31 (.12)
1963–66	1.98 (.29)	1.56 (.29)	0.86 (.27)	–0.28 (.71)	1.33 (.17)
1958–65	0.51 (.15)	0.54 (.14)	0.42 (.22)	–0.35 (.45)	0.42 (.10)
1966–69	2.89 (.33)	2.40 (.26)	2.59 (.36)	1.85 (.75)	2.53 (.18)
1969–70	2.81 (.72)	4.22 (.48)	4.03 (.58)	4.39 (1.29)	3.80 (.32)
Number of Observations	14	31	32	14	91
1970–73	12.56 (3.25)	9.58 (1.82)	4.86 (.55)	2.86 (.86)	7.34 (.87)
1966–73	7.47 (1.42)	5.83 (.70)	4.33 (.44)	2.54 (.73)	5.05 (.40)

CRQ is concentration ratio quartile.
Standard deviations are shown in parentheses.

Sources: Price Change 1958–73: *Wholesale Price Index, Industry Sector Price Indexes,* U.S. Bureau of Labor Statistics; Price Change 1954–58: *Census of Manufactures 1963,* vol. 4, Census Unit Value Indexes; Concentration Ratios: *Concentration Ratios In Manufacturing,* MC67(S)–2.1, U.S. Bureau of the Census.

Professor L. Weiss sought to determine the net effect of concentration on prices by adjusting for increases in the costs of labor and materials [33]. He found a zero or negative relationship, except for the period 1953–59, and if he had adjusted for changes in capital costs during this period his results probably would have agreed with his findings for other periods. A very comprehensive study of the relationship in Western European countries reached the same conclusion:

> Our analysis of Belgian, Dutch and French wholesale prices over the period 1958–1965 shows very clearly that . . . more-concentrated industries behaved exactly like less-concentrated industries. ([26], pp. 172–73).

The facts thus controvert the oft-repeated myth that inflation is caused by the price-raising activities of large firms in concentrated industries.

THE POLITICAL AND SOCIAL ARGUMENTS AGAINST LARGE FIRMS

Accumulating evidence flatly contradicts the *economic* argument that big enterprises and concentrated industries behave monopolistically and thereby damage the public interest. Such evidence supports the contrary view that competition is generally effective in oligopolistic industries, and that large firms enable society to benefit from important economies of scale. Of course, the dimensions of competition are much more numerous in such industries than are the simple price-and-output adjustments embodied in the classical model of atomistic competition. Real-world dynamic competition involves the variables of product quality, product performance, product financing and marketing, and many others, in addition to price. The planning and controlling activities of business firms represent efforts to adjust to external economic and market conditions, including the strategies of rival firms. The use of standard costing, target pricing, market share measurements, and similar practices are common to small and large firms, and are part of the competitive process rather than evidences of monopoly power [37].

But what reply should be made to those who advance *political and social* arguments against big businesses? Many concede that society benefits from the superior efficiency of large firms in concentrated industries, but hold that the political and social values of small businesses are more important. Some critics also contend that the existence of big businesses has led to the creation of big labor unions to countervail their economic power in collective bargaining.

The political and social attack on big business essentially reflects an antipathy for *all kinds* of large institutions in our populous, highly urbanized society. It is based on a nostalgic preference for the small-scale and simpler agrarian society of the nineteenth century. Although such a preference is understandable, it is simply unrealistic to believe in the possibility of recreating a small-scale rural society in the contemporary

United States. It would call for a radical restructuring not only of the business system but also of labor, educational, religious, and military institutions, not to mention government—which is the largest social institution of all! The inexorable fact is that great size and much concentration characterizes all kinds of institutions in U.S. society. And even were such a restructuring possible, it would be neither viable nor acceptable to the American people. The sacrifices in material standards of living and quality of life would be intolerable. And the loss of competitive strength in our relation with other nations that choose to retain the efficiencies of large-scale enterprises would be catastrophic.

PUBLIC POLICIES FOR LARGE FIRMS
AND CONCENTRATED INDUSTRIES

The imperatives of modern technology and of a large and growing human population *require* Americans, as well as the citizens of other advanced industrialized nations, to live in societies containing many large-scale institutions. These societies include vast business corporations, as well as national and international labor unions, great universities, huge military forces, and other large-scale organizations. But they will also include many medium and small enterprises, and other small-scale organizations. Institutions of all sizes have important—if different—economic and social roles to play in free societies.

Public policy should aim to foster the activities of private-sector institutions of all sizes, so long as they contribute to the general welfare. It should intervene to terminate, reform, or punish a private institution of any size only when it engages in antisocial behavior. The punitive power of government should not be used in a broad-scale attack on firms merely because they are large, or on industries simply because they are concentrated. Adherence to these fundamental principles would produce important changes in the policies and resource allocations of present U.S. antitrust programs. And if such changes were made, a material improvement could occur in business-government relationships, and in the ability of both institutions to enhance the well-being of the American people.

NOTES

1.   See, for example, Ralph Nader, "Introduction," *The Closed Enterprise System*, The Nader Study Group Report on Antitrust Enforcement, ed. Mark J. Green (Washington, D.C.: Center for the Study of Responsive Law, 1971).

2.   See W.G. Shepherd, *Market Power and Economic Welfare: An Introduction* (New York: Random House, 1970).

3. Blair [7] attributes inefficiency problems in the USSR and Yugoslavia to ubiquitous oligopoly. For a more balanced view see Adizes [2].

4. If managerial economies were the *sole* explanation of concentration, this theory would have to bear the burden of explaining why they are important in some industries, but not in others. More work needs to be done in this area. My present hypothesis is that managerial factors interact with plant scale economies, potentials for multiplant economies, and activities requiring the use of specialist or staff expertise in managing complex research, manufacturing, distribution, promotion, etc.

BIBLIOGRAPHY

1. Adams, Walter. "The Case for Structural Tests." *Public Policy Toward Mergers*. Edited by J.F. Weston and S. Peltzman. Pacific Palisades, Ca.: Goodyear, 1969.

2. Adizes, Ichak. *Industrial Democracy: Yugoslav Style*. New York: Free Press, 1971.

3. Bain, J.S. "Relation of Profit Rate to Industry Concentration: American Manufacturing, 1936–1940." *Quarterly Journal of Economics* 65 (August 1951): 293–324.

4. Bain, J.S. "Economies of Scale, Concentration, and the Condition of Entry in 20 Industries." *American Economic Review* 44 (March 1954): 15–39.

5. Bain, J.S. *Barriers to New Competition*. Cambridge, Mass.: Harvard University Press, 1956.

6. Bain, J.S. *International Differences in Industrial Structure*. New Haven: Yale University Press, 1966.

7. Blair, John M. *Economic Concentration: Structure, Behavior and Public Policy*. New York: Harcourt Brace Jovanovich, 1972.

8. Bock, Betty. *Statistical Games and the "200 Largest" Industrials: 1954 and 1968*. New York: The Conference Board, 1970.

9. Bock, Betty. "The Largest Companies and How They Grew." *The Conference Board Record* (March 1971).

10. Bock, Betty. "Dialogue on Concentration, Oligopoly, and Profit: Concepts vs. Data." *Conference Board Report No. 556* (1972).

11. Brozen, Yale. "The Antitrust Task Force Deconcentration Recommendation." *Journal of Law and Economics* 13 (October 1970): 279–92.

12. Brozen, Yale. "Bain's Concentration and Rates of Return Revisited." *Journal of Law and Economics* 14, 2 (October 1971): 351–69.

13. Brozen, Yale. "An Ivory Tower (Chicago) View of Advertising." Presentation before the AAA Eastern Annual Conference, New York, June 5, 1972.

14. Cohen, Kalman J. and Richard M. Cyert. *Theory of the Firm: Resource Allocation in a Market Economy*. 2d ed. Englewood Cliffs, N.J.: Prentice-Hall, 1975.

15. Comanor, W.S., and T.A. Wilson. "Advertising, Market Structure and Performance." *Review of Economics and Statistics* 49 (November 1967): 423–38.

16. de Podwin, H.J., and R.T. Selden. "Business Pricing Policies and Inflation." *Journal of Political Economy* 71 (1963): 110–27.

17. Demsetz, Harold. "Industry Structure, Market Rivalry, and Public Policy." *Journal of Law and Economics* 16(1) (April 1973): 1–9.

18. Engwall, Lars. "Industrial Concentration in Different Economic Systems." *Feitschrift-fur National Oconomie* 44 (December 1973): 449–60.

19. Grether, Ewald T. "Industrial Organization: Past History and Future Problems." *American Economic Review* 60 (May 1970): 83–99.

20. McGee, John 5. *In Defense of Industrial Concentration.* New York: Praeger, 1971.

21. Mann, H. Michael. "Seller Concentration, Barriers to Entry, and Rates of Return in Thirty Industries, 1950–1960." *Review of Economics and Statistics* 48 (August 1966): 296–308.

22. Mueller, Willard F. "Industrial Structure and Competition Policy." Studies by the staff of the Cabinet Committee on Price Stability. Washington, D.C., 1969, pp. 39–50.

23. Ornstein, S.I. "A Multiregression Analysis of the Concentration and Profits Relation." *Journal of Business* 45 (October 1972): 519–41.

24. Ornstein, S.I., R.E. Shrieves, M.D. Intriligator, and J.F. Weston. "Determinants of Market Structure." *Southern Economic Journal* 39 (April 1973): 612–25.

25. Pashigian, P. "The Effect of Market Size on Concentration." *International Economic Reivew* (October 1969): 291–314.

26. Phlips, Louis. *Effects of Industrial Concentration: A Cross-Section Analysis for the Common Market.* Amsterdam: North-Holland Publishing Co., 1971.

27. Pryor, Frederic L. "An International Comparison of Concentration Ratios." *Review of Economics and Statistics* 54 (May 1972): 130–40.

28. Rhoades, Stephen A. "Concentration, Barriers, and Rates of Return: A Note." *Journal of Industrial Economics* (November 1970).

29. Rosenbluth, G. *Concentration in Canadian Manufacturing Industries.* Princeton: Princeton University Press, 1957.

30. Shepherd, W.G. "Elements of Market Structure." *Review of Economics and Statistics* 14 (February 1972): 25–37.

31. Shepherd, W.G. "Elements of Market-Structure: An Inter-Industry Analysis." *Southern Economic Journal* 38 (April 1972): 531–37.

32. Singer, Eugene M. "Industrial Organization: Price Models and Public Policy." *American Economic Review* 60 (May 1970): 90–99.

33. Weiss, L.W. "Business Pricing Policies and Inflation Reconsidered." *Journal of Political Economy* 74 (April 1966): 177–87.

34. Weiss, L.W. "The Role of Concentration in Recent Inflation." Appendix to Statement of Richard W. McLaren before the Joint Economic Committee, July 10, 1970.

35. Weiss, L.W. "Quantitative Studies of Industrial Organizations." *Frontiers of Quantitative Economics.* Edited by Michael D. Intriligator. Amsterdam: North-Holland Publishing Co., 1971.

36. Weston, J. Fred. "Changing Environments and New Concepts of Firms and Markets." *New Technologies, Competition, and Antitrust.* New York: The Conference Board, 1970.

37. Weston, J. Fred. "Pricing Behavior of Large Firms." *Western Economic Journal* 10 (March 1972): 1–18.

38. Weston, J. Fred. "ROI as a Dynamic Management Control System." *Business Horizons* (August 1972).

39. Weston, J. Fred. "Business Power Over Markets and Consumers—The Facts." Chapter 20 in *Contemporary Challenges in the Business-Society Relationship,* edited by George A. Steiner. Los Angeles: UCLA Printing and Publication Department, 1972.

40. Weston, J. Fred and Stanley I. Ornstein. *The Impact of Large Firms on the U.S. Economy.* Lexington, Mass.: D.C. Heath, 1973.

41. Weston, J. Fred. "Discussion." *American Economic Review Proceedings* (May 1971): 125–27.

42. Weston, J. Fred. "Appraising Price and Pay Controls." Public Hearings of U.S. Price Commission, San Francisco, April 6, 1972, revised June 8, 1972.

43. Williamson, Oliver E. *Corporate Control and Business Behavior.* Englewood Cliffs, N.J.: Prentice-Hall, 1970.

44. Williamson, Oliver E. "The Vertical Integration of Production: Market Failure Considerations." *American Economic Review Proceedings* (May 1971): 112–23.

CHAPTER 4

Improving the Business-Government Relationship

Most participants in the seminar were preoccupied with ways and means of improving an unsatisfactory business-government relationship. No less than six of them made this the central theme of their papers. Their proposals involve alterations in the organizational structures and management policies of both governments and businesses. They encompass research to discover new knowledge, synthesis of existing knowledge, and educational programs to communicate this knowledge more widely.

Gilbert W. Fitzhugh offers a number of guidelines for the future relationship of business to government. In general, government's role is to make the rules and to create a favorable climate for private enterprise; the role of business is to produce the goods and services demanded in the market. The U.S. Constitution requires government to "promote" the general welfare—not to provide it. Fitzhugh is the retired Chairman of the Board of Directors and Chief Executive Officer of Metropolitan Life Insurance Company. Educated at Princeton University, he was a Fellow of the Society of Actuaries, and rose to the top position of his company in 1966. He is a leading student of social insurance, and in 1969 served as Chairman of a Presidential Panel on the Department of Defense.

W. Michael Blumenthal diagnoses the causes of the faulty operation of the American social system in recent years. He finds it due to accelerating social and technological changes that have magnified the complexity of our society, and to the growing interdependence of nations, which makes global solutions necessary. The issues deserving highest priority for study in his opinion include: redefining the role of business, designing forms of business-government collaboration on social projects, setting governmental standards for business behavior, educating leaders, financing political campaigns, and reforming the regulatory agencies. Blumenthal is Chairman of the Board of Directors and Chief Executive Officer of the Bendix Corporation. He was educated at the University of California and Princeton University, and he served as Deputy Assistant Secretary of State for Economic Affairs, and as Deputy Special Representative for Trade Negotiations under Presidents Kennedy and Johnson.

Alfred C. Neal *observes that the present structure and policies of govern-ment are woefully inadequate to perform the tasks that only government can perform. A fragmented U.S. government is threatening to destroy the integrated national markets that have been the wellspring of our productivity. And a prolif-eration of national governments threatens to fragment the world markets of mul-tinational business. Government structure is contradictory to the imperatives of business efficiency. And this problem is enhanced by the burgeoning size and the low productivity of governments. Reforms are imperative. Neal has served as President of the Committee for Economic Development since 1956. An economist by profession, he holds degrees from the University of California and Brown University, and he studied at the London School of Economics. Formerly Vice-President and Director of Research of the Federal Reserve Bank of Boston, he has served on several government commissions.*

Donald B. Rice *contends that there are large social payoffs to be gained by an expansion of research on public policies, their costs and their benefits. An example was the recommendation of the Rand Corporation to the City of New York that the most effective way to expand the housing supply was to conserve the existing stock (mainly by relaxing rent controls) instead of building additional units. He suggests that studies be made of ways to increase productivity and of the effects of wage-price controls. Also,* incentives *should be provided for effi-cient public administration and for innovative social thinking. President of the Rand Corporation since 1972, Rice is a former Assistant Director of the Office of Management and Budget. Educated at Notre Dame and Purdue Universities in management and economics, he has served as Deputy Assistant Secretary of Defense for Resource Analysis, where he earned the Meritorious Civilian Ser-vice Medal for contributions to the U.S. defense program.*

George A Steiner *expresses some of these same concerns. Steiner calls for cross-sectional research on business-government cooperation, including investi-gations: to identify major oncoming problems, to avoid abuses from antisocial collaboration, to provide incentives to action by business, and to ascertain public expectations about business-government collaboration. The most urgent subjects for business-government cooperation are, in Steiner's opinion, energy, urban transportation, and the rebuilding of cities. He sees an expanding field for such cooperation in what he describes as a "planning, but not a planned" society. Since 1956, Steiner has served as Professor of Management and Public Policy in the Graduate School of Management at the University of California, Los Angeles. He is also Director of its Center for Research and Dialogue on Busi-ness and Society. Educated at Temple University and the Universities of Penn-sylvania and Illinois, he was Director of Policy for the Office of Defense Mobili-zation during the Korean War, and later became Senior Economic Advisor of the Lockheed Aircraft Corporation. He has written extensively on corporate planning and on business-society relationships.*

Ralph Nader *focuses attention on the improvement of legal procedures as a means of enhancing the performance of government and its relationships with business and the public. In particular, he calls for more freedom of information, wider rights of citizens to challenge or to appeal court decisions, freer access to the legal system, a less secure and therefore a more responsible civil service, and safeguards against corruption. A lawyer by profession, he was educated at Harvard University. Nader has become nationally known as an advocate of citizen and consumer rights. He is the founder and Director of the Center for the Study of Responsive Law in Washington, D.C.*

GUIDELINES FOR FUTURE
BUSINESS-GOVERNMENT RELATIONSHIPS

Gilbert W. Fitzhugh

It is frequently observed that business should accept the fact that big government is here to stay, and should learn to live and cooperate with it. But cooperation is a two-way process. It is also important for the future of the United States that government cooperate with business. Both institutions rightfully share in the credit for the tremendous strides this country has made.

GOVERNMENTAL ACTIVITIES
PERVADE THE U.S. ECONOMY

Governments—federal, state, and local—play many roles in their relations with private enterprise. First, they are purchasers of more than one-fifth of the goods and services produced in our economy. All public expenditures, including not only goods and services but also transfer payments and other items, will run to nearly $440 billion in 1974, a staggering increase over the less than $2 billion spent at the turn of the century. With government playing an ever larger role, its influence over what will be produced, where it will be produced, and who will produce it, has permeated the economy.

In several states, much employment is generated by government contracts with private industry, in addition to the relatively large number of people directly on the payroll of governments in every state. Government participation is further manifested by its financial support of industry's research and development. Since our public school system began, government has played a major role in its operation and financing. In recent years, it has extended its activities to include aspects of the financing of college and university education.

The federal government is the nation's largest insurer, lender, and borrower. It is the largest landlord, the largest tenant, and the largest electric power producer. Almost every business decision is affected by the laws, regulations, or "voluntary guidelines" of some level of government. Under constant scrutiny, by one government agency or another, are wages and prices, employment practices, business investments, interest rates, and capital flows. One of the major questions needing study in depth is whether government operations have expanded so rapidly that they cannot be managed efficiently. Must they be contracted in order to become manageable?

Government alters market responses through subsidies, grants, investment credits, and depreciation allowances. Government holds itself responsible, rightly or wrongly, for levelling out the ups and downs of the economy, for maintaining a high employment level, for fostering a satisfactory rate of economic growth, for sustaining a sound dollar. In almost every industry, government looms increasingly large between the business firm and its customers, its employees, and its shareholders.

Government, like nature, abhors a vacuum. If there are legitimate needs that business or some other group does not meet, government will surely move in. Primarily, it is the demands of the American people that have pushed government into an ever-increasing role. The activities of government largely reflect the hopes and desires of the population. But the people may be uninformed or misinformed about the issues at stake; and some issues are so complex that it is extremely difficult to explain them. The complexity of our world has been multiplied by a tremendous increase in population, an enormous rise in knowledge and technology, and an incredible increase in the rate of change. These factors have revealed our lack of knowledge and our inability to resolve many problems.

Large as the federal government is, the vastness of state and local governments should not be overlooked. State and local expenditures are far greater than the civilian expenditures of the federal government, and they are growing much faster. The reasons are obvious: The shift of population to the metropolitan areas, the nation's growing commitments to education, ever-increasing industrialization, and secularly rising incomes. We have come to expect new parks, richer libraries, and improved minimum standards of living. The exodus to the suburbs of many middle- and higher-income families, coupled with the influx of lower-income families into the central cities, has inevitably increased the demands on state and local governments.

Some needs of state and local governments are met through federal grants. Unfortunately, grant programs are rarely stopped after the needs have been met. As a result, there are now hundreds of separate federal aid appropriations to state and local units. In addition to the waste from continuing unneeded grant programs, this diversity causes a heavy administrative burden and a lack of coordination, which, in itself, is costly. But general revenue sharing by the federal government, aimed at introducing some order into this area, raises a host of its own problems.

BUSINESS PRODUCES
WHAT THE COMMUNITY DEMANDS

The business community produces the goods and services and hence provides the jobs that make the economy function; and it builds the base for the tax revenues that fuel the operations of government. These must always be the primary objectives and responsibilities of business. Day-to-day business decisions and operations are vitally important to the economic strength of the country. In this highly scientific age business is the major instrument for the rising output of goods and services. Corporate decisions have far-reaching public effects, and businessmen have an obligation to make decisions in the public interest. By and large they do, because in our society there are few private interests that are wholly separate from the public interest. But the businessman must never forget his primary responsibility to run a successful enterprise.

Beyond its immediate responsibilities, business has become more and more involved with the community and with governments at all levels. Today, business is an active worker in programs for society. Many leading industries have increased their participation in community activities, seeking to foster the betterment of the areas in which they are located, for the sake of their own interests as well as for the civic good. Business participation in social problems at the state and federal levels includes participation in conferences on public issues, and active membership in numerous government commissions. It is an essential mechanism for dealing with the energy crisis and for improving the environment. Business has participated heavily in charitable, educational, training, and similar campaigns, both as contributors and as workers in the vineyards.

GUIDELINES FOR FUTURE
BUSINESS-GOVERNMENT RELATIONSHIPS

There are obvious and necessary roles in the economy that only government can fulfill. It must control the currency, and set up and enforce the rules of the economic game. It must be an impartial umpire to settle disputes, and a policeman to see that no party is taken advantage of.

Beyond that, our complex society has needs so large that they require community action. Roads and flood controls are examples. But we should not let government do things that private enterprise can do better. We should not assume that government officials alone have the social conscience to know what is best for the country. Nor should government be an active partner in making basic business decisions. Otherwise we would lose the tremendous vitality and adaptability that has made the American enterprise system the envy of the world. If government goes beyond the exhortation in the Preamble to the Constitution to *promote* the general welfare, and goes too far down the road to *providing* it, we will, for good or evil, be embarking on a whole new way of life.

Perhaps the most important function government could perform in the long run is to create a good climate in which business can prosper, grow, and provide employment. One of the most direct means would be to adopt a growth-oriented regulatory policy. Too many agencies with their often overlapping, cumbersome, and even contradictory or biased regulations, make business planning and decision making unduly difficult.

Tax policy is also of great importance because many business decisions are heavily based on their tax consequences. If tax laws and regulations were simplified and neutralized to permit decisions to be made primarily on the basis of productivity, the economy would benefit.

Governments should cooperate with, rather than hinder, the forces of free markets. Even though the interplay of free-market forces determines prices in most areas of the economy, government influence has expanded. A hard look at the many government programs subsidizing one sector of the population at the expense of others, or engaging in competition with private industry, is called for. Subsidies, once started, are continued long after their need may have disappeared. And new programs are continually added. To a maximum extent the free competitive market and not the government should allocate resources.

Furthermore, government regulations and programs should be constructive. They should promote incentive, initiative, and confidence in the private sector. Restrictions should be imposed only to the extent necessary to guard the public interest. For the efficient operation of a free economy, there must be a minimum amount of restraint and a maximum amount of freedom. Then business management can make innovative decisions that spur the economy. Wage, price, interest, and credit restraints, for example, bypass the market mechanism and make it difficult for both business and government to identify market pressures. Existing controls of this nature should be lessened or removed as rapidly as possible.

I remain unconvinced by those who say we must choose between high employment and growth in productivity on the one hand, and a stable price level on the other. We can and we must have both. In fact, over the long haul the only way we can have either is to have both. A choice is not only unnecessary, it is impossible. But it takes political courage to espouse this view. The forces behind inflation are the result of our collective actions, and they can only be stopped through our own actions. Whether or not we succeed in halting inflation depends on whether enough people think that the future economic health of the country is worth making painful decisions now—and are strongly motivated to make their views known.

The public interest and the business interest are the same in desiring certain qualities in a community. They all want health, safety, economic well-being, and dignity of person. When businesses seek plant sites they not only desire a ready source of labor and materials, but also a community in which the local government agencies are determined to promote a good climate for growth.

Businessmen must continue to be concerned with business-government interrelationships, by expressing their thoughts, ideas, and opinions. An able public affairs staff or an effective trade association is not enough. Executives must themselves be genuinely, deeply, and *personally* involved in public affairs. And it is not enough to offer criticisms; positive alternatives should be proposed.

One area in which business has a duty to exercise leadership is job training. Many jobs remain unfilled because qualified people cannot be found. Business should support all efforts to upgrade the educational level of the population, so that there will be adequately trained people to fill the jobs of the future. In one of the most sensitive areas of our society—adequate educational and job opportunities for minority groups—many corporations are now assuming an important role. Business can also make a real contribution to urban renewal, to the revitalization of our central cities, to pollution control, to health and welfare programs, to housing, to transportation, and to public safety programs.

Business must not only continue to do its job well, but it must also persuade the public that it is, in fact, doing so. In addition to making sure that its performance warrants approval, business needs to better communicate its goals and activities so that the public will understand and support it. There is an urgent need to project to more people a better knowledge of what makes the business system operate successfully. The business community and government have a common stake in expanding the economy and improving the quality of life. Cooperation between these two prime movers in our society is essential. Each should do what it does best. Cooperation, not partnership, should be the watchword. This *can* be achieved because both agree on the broad social objectives of the American society.

CORRECTING FLAWS IN THE BUSINESS-GOVERNMENT INTERFACE

W. Michael Blumenthal

THE TRADITIONAL AMERICAN CREDO

The main currents of American opinion have traditionally professed a major reliance upon private, profit-motivated initiative within a competitive environment to solve the problems of society. This, at least, has been the prevailing ethos since the founding of the Republic. One of our most deeply held beliefs has been that free enterprise is the best means of getting things done and achieving our social goals.

This faith in private initiative has been coupled with an almost instinctive suspicion and antipathy toward government in general, and big government in particular. Americans have turned to government for solutions to vital problems only at times of crisis and national emergency. They have continued to believe that "he governs best who governs least"; and that the less official interference, the better off the country will be.

Nor has this been simply a matter of method. Our most transcendent value, the freedom of the individual, has been equated with these two concepts—a free and unfettered system of private endeavor and the strictest possible limitation of government involvement in the citizen's affairs.

While this broad generalization about the way in which Americans have tended to look upon their society is certainly subject to considerable qualification, both in regard to areas of activity and periods of history, it is nevertheless true that this has remained to the present day the guiding principle in the conduct of our affairs. And if the results of the American system are measured against the actual performance of other modern industrial societies, we can conclude that the outcome has been relatively favorable. We have, of course, been blessed with great and rich resources. Nevertheless, we have been quite innovative in organizing and managing them, and we have led the world in achieving high levels of efficiency. We have managed to accumulate great wealth, while providing a relatively less uneven distribution of income than might have been expected. And, until recently, the system has been effective in satisfying the deep need and desire of Americans to live freely as individuals and to feel protected from the ubiquitous "dead hand" of the state.

CAUSES OF CONTEMPORARY UNCERTAINTY

The system has never worked perfectly; and during some periods of our history it has fallen far short of its potential performance. However, it is only in the last decade or so that Americans seem to have developed a growing feeling of uncertainty about the merits of our social system. A growing number of vital problems have remained unsolved, or have been dealt with inadequately. Mistrust of both government and business has grown. In the past, the basic system had been challenged only by dissident intellectuals and radical critics. Now skepticism and disaffection have become rife throughout the population.

This makes the issue of the proper roles of government and of private business—and of the relationship between the two—both timely and important. The context within which these issues need to be addressed evolves from the observation that our system has, in fact, been working less well in recent years. Too many problems have been ignored or dealt with inadequately; national priorities have remained unordered. Our faith in the ability of either government or business to deal with the country's vital needs has been shaken. Moreover, the interaction between these two major institutions has appeared to be increasingly inefficient, and not infrequently scandalous and corrupt.

What has caused the change? If it is true that the system has ceased to work well, how did this happen? Let us attempt to identify some of the major contributing factors to the current malaise in order to better define the areas that need investigation.

A few obvious reasons come quickly to mind. First, there has been a more rapid rate of social change in the postwar period than ever before. The rapidity of this change, the speed with which we are becoming an increasingly complex and technologically sophisticated society, has no doubt fundamentally altered the nature of our problems. Second, the interrelationships of the various nations of the world have become closer and more numerous during the past few decades, with the result that national solutions to more of the complex problems of society are no longer sufficient. Frequently, solutions must be fitted into a framework of relations with other national entities. These relationships are characterized by an unprecedented variety, mobility, and flow of communications. Other nations are struggling—as we are—with the baffling problems of reorganizing their societies to cope with modern reality. Problems of energy, of the environment, of access to and use of vital resources, illustrate the point.

These new factors, and many others that flow from them, have given rise to the present situation. They call for redefined business-government relationships. Many of our problems are similar to those of other industrial societies; and no doubt much can be learned from studying how other countries have attempted to deal with them. Indeed, there are some aspects of the organization and processes even of such alien societies as Soviet Russia and mainland China, which might have a limited applicability to the United States. Yet it would seem clear that we cannot pattern ourselves on any existing model. The American case is sui generis. Our history, traditions, needs, opportunities, and our position in the world, constitute a unique combination. The solutions to our problems, therefore, must also be unique.

HIGH PRIORITY ISSUES FOR STUDY

Among the many questions that might fruitfully be examined in a study of business-government relationships, the following appear to have special importance.

1. Redefining the Role of Private Business

The acceleration of change and the increasing complexity of social problems have brought a need to redefine U.S. business-government relationships. Business—especially big business—can no longer occupy an essentially separate part of the social spectrum with concerns and interests divergent from, if not antagonistic to, those of government. Traditional concepts lose much of their relevance in an age in which we are called upon to deal with such problems as conserving a healthy environment while vastly increasing our energy supplies. Government and business are now inextricably associated in dealing with social problems and in carrying out programs of broad scope. A whole new set of ground rules and relationships must be designed, based on a concrete study of the needs that must be met. Postwar developments have brought about a quantum jump in these relationships and have changed their very nature. Our society is now in a situation in which the attitudes and procedures of the past are no longer appropriate. Regulation, legislation, and, above all, the concrete conditions under which business and government can best collaborate on projects and programs designed to realize vital social objectives, should be the main subjects of such a study.

2. Collaborating on Social Projects

In an increasingly complicated world, public transportation, environmental needs, health services, defense, energy, and certain kinds of scientific and technological research require enormous resources that can be marshalled and mobilized only through government leadership. Gone forever are the days when such tasks could safely be left to resourceful entrepreneurs—to the Rockefellers, Harrimans, and Carnegies of a century ago. These programs involve fateful decisions with respect to national priorities, which a society like ours must make deliberately in light of its national goals. Business continues to have an essential role to play. First, by participating in the study and discussion that normally precede these decisions, and second, by helping to carry them out. Certain segments of government and business have already acquired experience in these cooperative ventures. We need to study this experience in order to determine whether we have devised the forms of collaboration best calculated to elicit the most creative and socially useful contribution from each of the partners.

3. Setting Standards of Business Behavior

Much of the criticism that is levelled against business for its failure to satisfy social needs or to meet its social responsibilities arises from unrealistic assumptions about how independently a single enterprise can operate in our present system. Faced with a multiplicity of pressures and frequently contradictory goals, the businessman runs a considerable risk of placing his enterprise at a competitive disadvantage if he acts independently in dealing with such problems as safety or pollution, or even in determining the percentage of his pretax profits he devotes to educational, cultural, or charitable works.

Society has vital needs that only the government can identify and assign priorities. We have ample evidence that the marketplace alone will not do it. The role of government, therefore, is to define the framework and to set the rules.

It goes without saying that business will have important inputs to contribute when the government undertakes to prepare its guidelines and to set its standards. The interaction between government and business in this area presents a problem, which would be profitable to study in terms of real and specific cases.

4. Educating for Leadership in
Business and Government

Competent people are needed to manage our affairs and to interact in the vastly changed business-government relationship that we can expect to develop in the years ahead. In the past, our best people have gravitated to private enterprise, which has had greater prestige. But the realtively high-quality persons that enter business—particularly the large corporations and the service professions—are still trained in narrow and limiting ways. They are ill-prepared to understand the new forms and levels of business-government relations, and the resulting problems that will materially affect our economy and our society as a whole. Relatively little opportunity and incentive are given to our ablest executives for interchange and lateral movement between business and government.

Other countries have dealt with this problem quite differently. In France, the great universities have attracted some of the best talent into the senior ranks of government administrators, creating an elite service whose members frequently move out into business organizations mid-stage in their careers. On the other hand, the French system doesn't provide much opportunity for the kind of short-stint government service that is common for a small number of relatively senior business and professional people in the United States. We can look at Japan, the Soviet Union, and other European countries for different patterns. We should, in any case, examine this question to see whether there are ways in which we can train the managers of business and government to have a better understanding of society's needs and to facilitate intelligent interaction between them.

5. Financing of Political Campaigns

Nothing more poisons, corrupts, and frustrates our efforts to achieve creative relationships between government and business than the present system of private contributions to finance candidates for political office. Unless we can remove this cancer from our system—a system in which both business and political leaders are prisoners—there is little hope of much progress in almost any other area. Difficult as the problems are, only public financing would seem capable of achieving this goal.

6. Auditing the Regulatory Agencies

Finally, we cannot undertake a systematic study of business-government relationships without taking a fresh look at the regulatory agencies. Many of them are hoary with age. They have been described as slow to act, frequently politicized at the top, and poorly staffed. It has also been charged that they tend to overlap in their jurisdictions, and to become the creatures of the industries they are supposed to monitor and control. The fact remains that the rapid transformation of our society has made the task of the regulatory agencies more complex, and potentially more important, than ever before. We should examine their role, especially in setting standards of business behavior, with a view to determining how this uniquely American phenomenon can make a more effective contribution.

FRAGMENTED GOVERNMENTS:
A ROADBLOCK TO SOCIAL PROGRESS

Alfred C. Neal

> Oh wad some power the giftie gie us
> To see oursels as others see us'
> It wad frae monie a blunder free us,
>   An' foolish notion.
>
> — *Robert Burns*

A group of American business executives and university scholars, and a Japanese counterpart group, have each recently made a study of the other's economy. The Japanese diagnosis of the U.S. economy can be summarized in a few quotations:

> The relatively low growth rate of the U.S. economy, combined with inflation in recent years, sharpened the problems of unemployment, poverty, and inequitable income distribution that had existed all along in the postwar period. The dominant belief in individualism and individual responsibilities and the fear of government encroachment upon individuals' rights and of government intervention in private economic activity led to the lack of appropriate public policy on such national problems as lags in industrial adjustment, deteriorating balance of payments, urban decay, environmental disruption, and the like.

> A series of factors are responsible for this slow growth in productivity, but the single most important one is associated with the lack of the organizational imperative of modern technology in the United States. This imperative appears in some other developed countries in the form of indicative planning, close collaboration between the public and private sectors, and/or various forms of far-reaching collaboration within the private sector itself. What they provide, above all, is the assurance that necessary complementary investments and government support will be forthcoming.[1]

GOVERNMENT INTERVENTION IN THE ECONOMY—AN HISTORICAL SKETCH

Government relates differently to business in the United States than it does in other countries. This unique American philosophy and practice has been responsible for much of the progress that has marked our history. In the period since the Civil War, it was only when the individualistic, competitive, self-adjusting market mechanism broke down that the U.S. government undertook to correct its most serious failings. Government strengthened the microeconomic mechanism by enacting antitrust laws and by regulating "natural monopolies" in the quarter century centered on 1900. It undertook macroeconomic intervention beginning in the 1930s, and completed the machinery in 1946 with the Employment Act.

Despite some awkward attempts of government to intervene in the economy in previously untried ways during the early 1930s, we came to put our faith in the use of macroeconomic instruments for restoring and maintaining economic growth. These instruments have been fiscal and monetary policies which, when used properly and in combination, have demonstrated sufficient success that it would be rash, indeed, to question their value. That the U.S. economy has not had noninflationary economic growth is not the fault of the instruments but of their misuse and of their frustration by other policies.

When, for the first time within the memory of those now framing public policy, the United States encountered a severe balance-of-payments problem in 1971, we first exhausted all of the instruments designed to palliate a fundamental disequilibrium and then resorted to still another macroeconomic instrument. That instrument was a floating exchange rate, which, although much better suited to smaller countries than to our own, quickly became subject to management.

But macroeconomic instruments alone, even if properly used, would have been insufficient to keep the economy viable and healthy. The system's benefits were not well-distributed and too many people were left stranded. We still relied upon an essentially unguided system for allocating resources and for determining the distribution of income. While this reliance was generally correct in the sectors and for the people that were its victims, it created strong antagonisms and demands for reform. In consequence, we adopted a system of social security for the aged and retired. We supplemented this with a welfare program and unemployment compensation.

Believing that unequal education was not consistent with the national ethic, we began to support education on a large scale and with untold waste. We adopted training programs for the poorly educated, and retraining for those whose jobs and skills had become obsolete, with still more waste. Finally, we recognized the damage being done by treating the environment as a free good, and we undertook *ad hoc* programs of environmental improvement that began to become effective just in time to contribute to an energy shortage.

The foregoing sketch of the impingement of government policy on the economy recalls the faltering steps that Americans have taken under the most urgent pressures to correct failures in the economy by using the instruments of government. Let us turn now to the question of whether the United States has a structure of government adequate to the new tasks that only governments can perform.

AN OBSOLETE STRUCTURE OF
U.S. GOVERNMENT

Ours is a federal system in which powers are divided among national, state, and local governments and, within the national government, among the legislative, executive, and judicial branches. Inasmuch as this system has survived for nearly 200 years, one must be cautious in faulting it. Nevertheless, an objective appraisal leads to the conclusion that the forms and instruments of government for dealing with contemporary economic problems are woefully inadequate to the tasks that they are called upon to perform. Successive adaptations by court decisions have kept the governmental system going, and have even enabled it to provide tolerable services. But differences among the laws and regulations of the fifty states and the thousands of local governments are imposing increasingly difficult burdens on national business enterprises. And these subsidiary governments have proven inadequate to deal with the newer problems of the modern industrial state.

State jurisdiction over welfare payments, for example, despite rising federal intervention, has produced such wide differentials between the richer and the poorer states as to foster a migration of indigent persons to the central cities of the industrial North and West. Because of debilitating slums, illiteracy, and crime, business and the middle class have fled the central cities at a rapid rate, compounding the energy shortage and degrading the environment.

Deficiencies in health, in education, in training, and in labor market organization, have contributed to a persistently high rate of unemployment, even in an inflated economy, and of disaffection among the less privileged who are increasingly concentrated in urban areas. The absence of a national labor market has resulted in high rates of unemployment in some areas, while jobs go begging in others. Finally, we have adopted a federal system of environment control that violates the reasonable principle that the quality of the environment in different regions of the country ought to be subject to standards meaningful to the people who live there. Instead, federal policies frequently deny influence to regional majorities. Real influence consists mainly of small minorities exercising veto power over projects that would be beneficial to the majority of the people in a region. Examples are the siting of power plants and oil refineries, the development of deep-water ports, offshore oil drilling, the Alaska pipeline, and surface mining of coal.

Unfortunately, the fiasco of environmental control, from which we will be suffering for many years, does not conclude this somber list of failures attributable to inadequate government structures. Laws and regulations controlling business have multiplied in the fifty states and in thousands of local jurisdictions as well as within the federal government. In consequence, this nation, whose productivity has grown phenomenally because of mass production for its large national market, is now *threatened by market fragmentation* in the name of health, safety, environmental improvement, or some other worthy cause.[2]

THE PROLIFERATION OF NATIONAL GOVERNMENTS

The spectacle of fragmented and conflicting governments does not end at our national boundaries. The multinational corporation, which has brought to the world the benefits that the national corporation of earlier decades brought to the United States, is now faced with that same proliferation of governments and market fragmentation. A peculiar American contribution to the world has been the basically democratic and highly laudable goal of self-determination. It was carried forward by U.S. leadership in the postwar world, and the United States became the principal architect of a world full of new governments created in the American image. Fifty-one governments established the United Nations in 1945; presently, there are nearly three times that many member countries. Each exercises full sovereignty, maintains international representation, and has a superstructure of government that intervenes in the economic affairs of its own country and internationally to the extent of its interests and abilities.

The consequences of a proliferation of national governments in the world are potentially more serious than are the consequences of a proliferation of local governments in the United States. National governments exercise the power of life or death over the private business firm. They possess the power to control a strategic raw material, as we see today in the case of petroleum. The powers of national governments to set standards for products, to control business practices, to give preferences to their own nationals, and to exercise discrimination in the taxation of business, are all beyond the review of any recognized international tribunal having jurisdiction or power to enforce its decisions.[3] Perhaps most serious of all is the conflict of laws that results when a company must violate the laws of one country in order to observe the laws of another. Although this case is classic in the area of antitrust, prior to the re-establishment of U.S. relations with the Soviet Union and China, it reached nearly tragic dimensions in the conflict over the sale of strategic goods and services.

The salient point is that *the structure of governments in our own country and in the world has grown increasingly contradictory to the imperatives of efficiency and profitability in serving markets,* which is the dominant motive of the modern business system.

THE LOW PRODUCTIVITY OF
GOVERNMENTS

But beyond this contradiction—which makes the classic Marxian contradiction look like a schoolchild's exercise—is the burden imposed by the unmitigated growth of government. Employment in government and nonprofit services has been growing nearly twice as fast as employment in the economy as a whole. There is now one job in government for every four in the private sector. The proportion of the gross national expenditure accounted for by governments in the United States is nearly one-third; and some Western European countries have even higher ratios.

If the increasing proportion of governmental to total expenditures were merely a reflection of the public's choice of collective over private goods and services, one could conclude that this phenomenon was simply a matter of taste and of political philosophy. But it is far more than this; it represents the encroachment of the less productive sectors of the economy upon the most productive sectors.[4] Some encroachment results from an unnecessary overlapping of services which is the consequence of the proliferation of governments. The major part, however, is the consequence of the lesser productivity of government than of the private sector. Government leaders get elected and stay in office by providing jobs (whether they are worth the cost or not) and by sponsoring programs that provide services to people (whether efficiently or not). As government is now structured, it operates under a logic antithetical to that of the private sector. Under present conditions, proliferating governments and increasing government expenditures are slowing the growth of our nation's productivity and of our standard of living.

How could business leaders—particularly those of the large national and multinational companies—have permitted the development of governmental structures so inappropriate to the future health and growth of the economy? That such structures exist is a convincing refutation of the Marx-Lenin thesis that business in a capitalist system controls the governmental superstructure. When life was simpler, governments smaller, and business less subject to law and conscience, business did for a time exert sufficient influence over government to feel confident of government beneficence. And, in some places, some companies still exercise extensive political influence in their own self-interest. As recently as 1972, some companies were induced to make presidential campaign contributions in expectation of favors, only to subsequently learn that competitors had also bought into a zero-sum game; favors to all is favors to none!

Business now realizes that its political position is that of a minority, and that other institutions, especially unions, can exert far superior political influence. It has yet, however, to identify itself firmly with the broad public interest movements seeking to clean up the election system and to reform the archaic structures and processes of government. Only when these steps have been taken can business expect to enter into a meaningful and mutually advantageous partnership with government.

The greatest problem in business-government relations is that of *perception*—perception that the beneficent self-adjusting world of our earlier history and later nostalgia does not exist, that much of our intellectual capital and social philosophy is obsolescent, and that the institutions and skills needed to cope with the world as it is are not yet invented. The first priority in business-government relations is to create an understanding that a partnership of business and government is a necessary condition for achieving individual and social objectives. But an effective partnership is impossible unless governments can be reformed to make business a symbiont, rather than a guest invited to dinner to find that *he* is it!

NOTES

1.   From a manuscript prepared by Keizai Doyukai, Tokyo, Japan, 1973.

2.   A current local example, which must have many counterparts elsewhere, is the urgent request of Consolidated Edison to convert two New York City power plants back to coal. This move was advocated by the federal energy office, denied by the New York City environmental protection agency, and granted by the New York State agency; new appointees in the latter two agencies have indicated they will reverse their predecessors, thus maintaining the contradiction. The hundreds of thousands of people and the firms in this utility's service area, but outside the city, have no voice in a decision that will greatly affect their jobs and well-being.
Another striking example is the division of pollution control of the Hudson River between state authorities in New York and New Jersey; each has jurisdiction from its own shore to the middle of the river!

3.   Saudi Arabian interruption of oil shipments to the United States during 1974 was in violation of a treaty between the two countries and is a case in point.

4.   This does not imply that government is nonproductive; it refers to the well-known low or zero rate of growth in productivity in most government services.

THE POTENTIALITIES OF
PUBLIC POLICY RESEARCH

Donald B. Rice

The old story about how porcupines make love—very, very carefully—aptly describes the traditional relationship between business and government in the United States. This prickly affinity between our two dominant social institutions has produced both public goods and public bads. Let us single out a few issues that arise from this ambiguous business-government relationship and then try to point the way toward a socially more fruitful cohabitation. In particular, we shall address attention to (1) the need for business involvement in public policy research, (2) the prospect for improved understanding of the workings of the U.S. economy and of the impacts of governmental policies, and (3) the opportunity for increasing the private role in supplying public goods and services.

THE ECOLOGY OF PUBLIC POLICY ANALYSIS

A distinguishing characteristic of our complex society is the interdependence of its parts. It is scarcely an exaggeration to say that everything is related to everything else. While it broadens our sense of membership in a larger human community, this interdependence also intensifies conflicts of values and goals, both public and private. Collective and individual decisions have consequences that impinge on a multitude of interests. One result of this diversity of interests is a blurring of the traditional boundaries between the public and private sectors.

For example, no action—or inaction—on the part of government in such diverse areas as the environment, communications, transportation, energy, urban development, or international economic policy, can fail to affect interests in the private sector. And conversely, we are becoming more aware of the spillover effects of private activities that affect the public interest, such as environmental pollution, job and housing discrimination, natural resource development, and even the design of automobiles.

What does this interdependence mean for public policy? For one thing, it means that we must attempt to maximize our knowledge of the available alternatives before making a far-reaching decision; and we must predict as accurately as possible the consequences of our actions. The increasing complexity of society has made it impractical and even dangerous to rely solely on intuition or past experience. Intuition tends to break down when it confronts systems that are more complex than those our everyday experience exposes us to. Policies can produce consequences that are exactly the opposite of those that were intended. Nearly all social issues can benefit from increased information about policy choices and their consequences. Over the past two decades, techniques have evolved that can illuminate problems marked by great uncertainty, competing alternatives, large costs, and far-reaching consequences. These techniques are applicable to *public policy research.*

Public policy research is a practical philosophy for problem solving that deals with complex issues affecting public and private interests where efficiency is not the only criterion of a feasible solution. It attempts to provide the decision maker with information, based upon an analysis of policy alternatives, in a decision environment characterized by multiple interests, vague or conflicting objectives, and a strong interaction between means and ends. It builds our stock of knowledge about public choices, both of ends and of means.

An actual example will illustrate the process of public policy research. Several years ago the Rand Corporation set out to assist the City of New York with some of its urban administration problems. Specifically, we at Rand were asked to find a cheaper and faster way of providing public housing. Construction targets were not being met, and the clamor for additional housing was increasing rapidly.

As our studies progressed, we became convinced that the traditional emphasis on *new* construction was unserviceable. We came to believe that the attention of city officials should be focused instead on saving the *existing* stock from the growing threat of deterioration and abandonment, and that solutions should be sought on a citywide scale. Most owners of rent-controlled housing were not getting enough revenue to maintain their buildings properly and still earn a reasonable return on capital. As a result, this housing stock was deteriorating at rates that would swamp any feasible amount of new construction. The solution was not to turn the faucet on harder; it was to plug the drain. After a lengthy process of persuasion and additional analysis, the city officials were convinced that the original goal of new construction was simply not feasible, and that the objective should be shifted to preservation of existing housing. Among other measures, changes in the existing rent-control laws were finally accepted by the city and have now been implemented.

This example illustrates two important features of public policy research: (1) *both* means and ends are subjected to careful analysis; and (2) policy research really *does* promote positive change.

The analytical tools of public policy research have come into fairly widespread use in the federal government; and this is a healthy development. However, the sponsorship and performance of public policy research is too important to be left to the government. The private sector possesses the capability to perform public policy research. Private research institutions have made unique contributions to the rational resolution of public issues, and the government has relied heavily on research recommendations from nonprofit research corporations, universities, and even profit-seeking companies. The private sector has a large stake in public policies, and shortfalls in knowledge are a continuing deterrent to good public policy. The capability for policy research exists and is understood; but so far the sponsorship and utilization of public policy research has only been undertaken by government, with some assistance from private foundations. The missing ingredient would seem to be business sponsorship of public policy research.

Business can realize several benefits from sponsorship of public policy research. These include attention to topics of special concern to business where government has lesser concern; increased knowledge in areas that don't fit neatly into the charter of any one government agency; assurance of the independence of private research institutions; and greater confidence that government policies will be decided on the basis of foreknowledge of their consequences.

The business community should recognize that a competent resolution of policy issues is in everyone's interest. The policies and programs of government have far-reaching impacts, consuming resources and human talents that are often in short supply. It is therefore imperative that government undertake only those programs most likely to work—whose goals are most attainable and are achievable in the most equitable and efficient manner possible. Business can enhance this process by supporting the kinds of independent and objective analyses that the private research institutions are uniquely equipped to provide.

A BETTER KNOWLEDGE BASE
FOR ECONOMIC POLICY

A more fruitful interaction between the public and private sectors would be fostered by the creation of new knowledge about the workings of the U.S. economy. Let us focus briefly on two issues of current interest: (1) increasing the productivity of the national economy, and (2) learning from our recent experiments with wage and price controls.

1. A dominant factor in the attainment of our present standard of living has been the long-term growth of industrial productivity. The precise explanation of this growth, however, has proven elusive. Quality of labor, amount of capital investment, and efficiency of management have all been cited. Part of the difficulty lies in the measurement of both outputs and inputs. Further, in a diversified market economy,

meaningful aggregation of data across firms and across industries is difficult. When we look at the historical growth of the U.S. economy from an international perspective, however, especially in comparison with that of the less-developed countries, what stands out is the central role of *knowledge,* as embodied in technical progress. It seems to be the creation and diffusion of new knowledge, as reflected in all the factors of production, that stimulates shifts in the production curve.

Although it is fairly clear that technological progress is the prime determinant of the rate of growth in productivity, there is much that we do not yet understand. We do not know nearly enough about how new knowledge is generated, how it penetrates the economy, and what we can do to stimulate this process. The optimum conditions for the generation of new knowledge and its application to production are subjects deserving close study. One recent economic analysis, for example, suggests that a clear distinction must be made between the environment conducive to the production of new knowledge and the organization of business that can rapidly reap the full benefits of its use. This distinction raises issues regarding the role of research and development in the generation of basic knowledge and new technology, the responsibility of government in promoting research, the most efficient ways of making new technology available, and the creation of incentives for its speedy adoption by industry. It also raises fundamental questions about ways of regulating the economy in the interest of stimulating research and development. Up to a certain point, economies of scale seem to be effective in generating new technology; after this point, these economies decline rather rapidly. Since much basic technology has important positive spillover effects for the economy as a whole, this phenomenon poses important challenges for antitrust policy.

A subject of increasing concern is the productivity of the service sector. Sometime during the last decade and a half, the U.S. economy became the first in history in which more than 50 percent of the labor force was engaged in providing services rather than in the production of tangible goods. Today, two thirds of the work force is employed in service industries, and by 1980 the figure will be close to 80 percent. What are the long-term implications of this trend for productivity?

It is clear that the problems of measuring productivity in the goods-producing sector are compounded in the service sector. Apart from the intrinsic difficulties of measuring output per teacher-hour or per physician-hour, for example, the consumer also plays an important role in service productivity. As Victor Fuchs has pointed out, the consumer actually works in the supermarket, the laundromat, and the bank: "Productivity in banking is affected by whether the clerk or the customer makes out the deposit slip—and whether it is made out correctly or not."[1] A full analysis must take these relationships into account.

Employment in government now encompasses more than a quarter of employment in the service sector; and all components of government employment have grown more rapidly in the last twenty years than has the total labor force. Here, problems of output measurement become especially acute. If, as William Baumol has suggested, wages in the labor-intensive service sector tend to parallel those in the technology-intensive goods-producing sector, the low growth of productivity in government can have important implications for government finance and for price inflation in the economy.[2] Without an intensive effort to increase productivity in the service sector—including the public sector—the prospects may be for a slower growth of national productivity.

2. Another issue of economic policy concerns the recent experience with wage-price controls by the federal government. It appears that the original goals of the 1971–73 wage and price controls were not met.[3] The fact that the Phase I wage and price "freeze" was relatively effective can probably be attributed to its brief duration. Moreover, the market dislocations caused by continuing controls have in some cases been severe; they partly account for acute shortages of some goods and materials. It is clear that price controls have exacerbated the energy shortage, for example. Until we are able to incorporate the lessons of such experiences into our policymaking, we seem fated to repeat the errors of the past. It is clear that we need a much better understanding of the proper role of the federal government in managing the economy.

The U.S. economy has entered a period of traumatic and far-reaching changes. We seem to be moving from an era of cheap and plentiful resources to a time of relative scarcity. It would be dangerously misleading to conceive our present troubles in terms of crisis, treatment, and recovery. In medicine, a crisis is a state from which the patient either recovers or dies. Neither outcome is likely in the present case, for the malady is not acute, but chronic. Until we can undertake a long-range reordering of our economic priorities in both the public and private sectors, we will be in the position of the physician who treats the symptoms rather than the underlying pathology.

THE "REPRIVATIZATION" OF PUBLIC SERVICES

Another aspect of public policy in need of study is the potential opportunity for private organizations to participate in the delivery of public services.

Over the past four decades, increasing demands have been made on government to address a host of public problems. One result has been the rapid increase of employment in the public sector. In part this growth seems to have become a self-generating process, in the sense that our discovery of new social problems has paralleled the growth of the problem-solving activities of government. But the performance of government has not matched its good intentions. Too many expensive social programs have been launched on too slender a foundation of administrative competence and empirical knowledge. The outcome has been a waste of resources, disappointed hopes, and an erosion of public confidence. We must find a more effective way of seeking and implementing solutions to public problems.

There are two distinct needs. The first is to provide *incentives for efficient administration* of public programs. The bureaucracy is a money-consuming institution, and the traditional measure of public programs has been monetary input rather than real social output. More important, bureaucracy can also be viewed as a budget-maximizing institution in which incentives are oriented as much toward obtaining an annual budgetary increment as toward minimizing the cost of current operations. This is simply the value engendered by the bureaucratic institutional environment.

The second need is to provide *incentives for innovative thinking* about social problems. The confidence, not to say hubris, with which the government launched many of the social welfare programs of the 1960s has been largely dissipated; the catalogue of its program failures is well-known. Many approaches to social ills that were successful under the conditions of the New Deal have been mechanically, and inappropriately, applied to new problems in new social and economic circumstances. Because it is essentially a preserving and protecting institution, government is not adept at innovation. Nor does it provide adequate incentives for the efficient management of ongoing programs and services.[4]

The evidence suggests that most of the modern innovations in organization and management have arisen in response to competitive pressures in the private sector. If we are to stimulate the production of new ideas on public policy and to minimize waste in their execution, we might explore the possibility of transferring some of these problem-solving activities to the competitive arena. What I am suggesting is what Peter Drucker has termed the "reprivatization" of some of the operations of government.[5]

The business community's increasing recognition of its social responsibilities is a healthy development. But much of this socially beneficial activity is, quite naturally, a by-product of business's profit-making activities. What is needed is more direct participation by the private sector as an instrumentality of public choice. Whether this activity would be best conducted by profit-making or nonprofit organizations is perhaps a moot issue. The crucial element is a fruitful separation of the necessary decision-making functions of government from the process of innovation and implementation.[6]

What kinds of activities might be more efficiently performed by the private sector? The design, evaluation, and administration of welfare programs might be candidates. There are even more obvious candidates: the operation of the government's uranium enrichment facilities; the provision of municipal services such as fire protection . . . refuse collection and disposal; or the conduct of routine administrative services at all levels of government.

There is no mechanical procedure for deciding which activities might be more effectively and efficiently performed by the private sector. Such questions could be partly decided by the organizational resources available. Small-scale experimentation over a range of services now administered by government would help to provide some answers. But an optimal division of labor between business and government requires that we reconsider their proper spheres of competence.

NOTES

1. Fuchs, Victor. "The First Service Economy." *The Public Interest* (Winter 1966); *The Service Economy.* National Bureau of Economic Research, Inc., and Columbia University Press. 1968.

2. Baumol, William J. "Macroeconomics of Unbalanced Growth: The Anatomy of Urban Crisis." *American Economic Review* (June 1967).

3. Boissevain, H., ET AL. "The Effectiveness of Phase II Price Controls." P-5045. The Rand Corporation (July 1973). Also Feige, Edgar L., and Douglas K. Pierce. "The Wage-Price Control Experiment—Did it Work?" *Challenge* (July/August 1973).

4. Boulding, Kenneth. "Interview." *Challenge* (July/December 1973).

5. Drucker, Peter. "The Sickness of Government." *The Public Interest* (Winter 1969).

6. Kennedy, C., and A. P. Thirall. "Technical Progress: A Survey," *The Economic Journal* (March 1972).

CREATING A COOPERATIVE INTERFACE BETWEEN BUSINESS AND GOVERNMENT

George A. Steiner

American society now confronts socioeconomic problems of great and increasing complexity, the resolution of which requires much closer cooperative relationships between business and government than we have ever known. Unfortunately, our past experience has not generated the philosophy, the policies, or the techniques that are needed to guide such a relationship. In this paper I am proposing measures to overcome these obstacles, while at the same time avoiding certain social disadvantages that close cooperation could bring.

BARRIERS TO BUSINESS-GOVERNMENT COOPERATION

Effective cooperative efforts by business and government in the United States are inhibited, in the first place, by philosophical attitudes that are more negative than positive. An antipathy has always existed between people in the two institutions that has hampered close working relationships. Major exceptions to this hostility occurred during World War II and the Korean War, although some mutual distrust continued in both instances. This antipathy has been buttressed by a persistent business philosophy, rooted in classical laissez-faire economics, of "government hands off business."

A stance of aloofness still inhibits close cooperative efforts in dealing with national problems. Many view closer working relationships between business and government with alarm. Some fear that the result will be more business influence on government; others fear that government will dominate business. Still others see such a development as reinforcement of the monolithic business-government power that already dominates our society. But, since we must have closer coordination between business and government to solve our major problems, these older philosophies must be changed.

A second major obstacle is the inability of government officials to foresee major emerging problems and to take the necessary action to forestall or soften crises before they strike. The energy problem is a classic illustration. Typically, in the past, we have allowed events to reach crisis proportions, and then tried to deal with them by throwing money at them. As problems become more numerous and more complex it is folly to persist in this pattern of behavior. We must anticipate future problems and make plans to cope with them.

A third barrier to closer cooperation between business and government is that there is no suitable body of tested principles and practices to guide the relationship. We lack appropriate methods to define the real nature of a problem, to set goals, to analyze alternatives, to develop policies and programs, and to measure results. We have had close business-government cooperation in the past principally in the areas of developing space vehicles and military equipment. A comparable cooperative effort will be increasingly needed in civilian programs during the years ahead.

Programs of research and dialogue, initiated and supported by the Norton Simon Commission, can help overcome these deficiencies and permit the nation to benefit from closer business-government cooperation. This can be done while avoiding the abuses that uncontrolled business-government cooperation could engender. The proposed programs should embrace both cross-sectoral research and research on specific functions and problems.

CROSS-SECTIONAL RESEARCH ON
BUSINESS-GOVERNMENT COOPERATION

There is a broad spectrum of possible business-government cooperation. At one end of the spectrum are joint ventures carried out by public-private corporations such as COMSAT. Still relatively close, but less intimate, relationships are involved in such projects as the NASA Apollo program. At the other end of the spectrum are contractor relationships for products made by businesses which business had little or no part in designing—the firms' managers merely responding to a profit incentive. We are here concerned mainly with types of close cooperation near the former end of the spectrum. In the development of business-government joint ventures in the future, four problems range horizontally across the field, requiring research and illumination.

First, there is need for systematic examination of the future to *identify major problems* affecting the business-government interrelationship which, if delineated, would trigger current actions. The government from time to time has tried to do this. Thus, the Paley Commission attempted during the 1950s to assess raw material requirements. Also, some years ago the Joint Economic Committee tried to determine the dimensions of the potential imbalance in the energy demand-supply relationships. In both cases major problems were forecast; but in neither case did the studies stimulate current actions to cope with the future problems they identified. Private corporations also systematically scan the future in their long-range planning programs, but the results are not ordinarily the subject of discussion with the government.

The Norton Simon Commission could improve the process by which government surveys the future and translates its findings into better current decisions. It could support "futures" research outside government. The findings could be widely disseminated, and could become the subject of further research to devise ways of stimulating current actions if important problems were foreseen. For example, if it is perceived that American business in the years ahead is not likely to finance basic research to the degree necessary to lift productivity and to develop new technology, what actions should government undertake now to cope with this deficiency? These findings could be the subject of dialogue among researchers, government officials, and business managers. The more light thrown on such issues, the more likely it will be that timely remedial actions will be taken by government, and by business as well.

Second, we should investigate ways to *avoid abuses* that can develop when business and government cooperate closely. Experience has shown that, under such conditions, business can exert excessive influence on government (e.g., the ICC and the railroads). On the other hand, business-government cooperation can severely hamper business. Government can dominate managerial decisions in the private sector. It can, by virtue of its monopsonistic position, squeeze profits to a subnormal level. It can foster inefficient productive methods through a poor choice of incentives. The aerospace industry is filled with illustrations of such problems, and its record should be fully examined. The aim is to identify policies and procedures that will avoid bad outcomes in future business-government undertakings. The Commission should also support research that attempts to develop measures of performance for business-government cooperative efforts.

Third, research is needed on *incentives* for business. The profit-and-loss discipline of private enterprise could be a powerful force for the efficient execution of programs desired by government. As government and business join hands in dealing with societal problems, the strength of their motivation should be enhanced and maintained. There are many ways to achieve this. The mixture of techniques that provides the greatest incentive for effective response will vary across the spectrum of cooperation. The problem of defining the best mix could be researched alone or in conjunction with each area of business-government cooperation.

Fourth, research is required to identify *the particular fields* in which the public expects business and government to *cooperate.* Society expects much more from its institutions today than it did in the past. Business is now being asked to help resolve major social problems, such as environmental pollution, and to improve the quality of life. Government is expected to establish the proper standards for achieving societal goals and to take direct action. Where appropriate, business and government are expected to form a partnership rather than deal with each other at arms' length, as classical philosophy required. The scope and thrust of society's expectations deserve more attention than they have yet received.

HIGH PRIORITY SUBJECTS OF BUSINESS-GOVERNMENT COOPERATION

Increasing business-government coordination to meet society's goals is required most urgently in the fields of energy, transportation, and city rebuilding (especially of low-income housing). Other subjects requiring attention in the near future include ocean mining, multinational corporate dealings with host governments, technology transfer to underdeveloped countries, rehabilitation of depressed regions in the United States, and nondefense research and development.

The energy problem will not be resolved quickly. The United States can become energy-independent within the next ten years only with close coordination of business-government planning and operation. Modernizing and integrating our transportation systems is a staggering task that also involves the closest relationship between business and government. For years, governments have spent billions of dollars on the problem with no acceptable solution in sight. In city rebuilding, and provision of low-income housing, dollar expenditures have been even greater, and probably less successful, in terms of goal achievement.

Each of these areas poses the following fundamental issues for research:

1. What are alternative ways to measure the real dimensions of the problem?
2. What are alternative organizational techniques to deal with the problem? For example, is a public-private corporation the best method, or should the public-private sectors cooperate in other ways?
3. What are the respective roles of business and government? Generally speaking, government should assume a *policy* role, choose incentives for the private partner, and determine how the entire operation shall account for its performance. The private sector should be responsible for aid and counsel to the government in discharging its functions, but should employ its skills primarily in *implementing* overall policy established by government.
4. What *incentives* should be provided to business in the best interests of business, government, and society?
5. How shall business be held *accountable* for its performance? What reporting mechanisms are preferred? What measures will be used to evaluate performance? Who will evaluate performance?

These are extremely difficult questions, the answers to which are not apparent. A major responsibility of the researchers should be to recommend new, imaginative, and innovative answers.

TOWARD A PLANNING— NOT A PLANNED—SOCIETY

Business today is moving into social fields as a result of government demands and also as a voluntary response to societal expectations. Government is using market incentives to induce business involvement in social programs. Beyond this, society expects these two powerful institutions to cooperate in using their talents to meet and resolve major socioeconomic problems. The two will surely move closer together in the future. If we drift into this partnership without careful thought, we may miss a great opportunity for effective cooperation. The Norton Simon Commission can make an important contribution to society by supporting research and action programs on the conditions for effective cooperation.

This is not a call for a planned society—for some new form of socialism. What is proposed is a new partnership of the public and private sectors, designed to resolve, better than in the past, the great socioeconomic problems that face us now and that will appear more frequently and in more complex forms in the future. The result we seek is not a planned but a planning society.

LEGAL PROCEDURAL GAPS
AND THE RELATIONSHIP

Ralph Nader

One way to improve the business-government relationship is to assure that the *procedures* used by government in dealing with each facet of the relationship contribute to democratic, wise, and efficient public policies. The facets of the relationship are, of course, numerous. They include taxing, regulating, subsidizing, contracting, licensing, leasing, and promoting; setting of standards for products, markets, and competition; and regulating the "claimant process," which includes lobbying, conflicts of interest, and rights of appeal. Irrespective of the intrinsic merits of any particular federal government program, however, *uniform* procedures should be used in carrying out each program, if those affected—whether organized or unorganized—are to have opportunity for expressing their views and are to be treated equitably.

FREEDOM OF INFORMATION

Freedom of information is basic to any quest for procedural due process—and to prevent the preferential access to information that is often a source of corruption between a governmental agency and its clientele. Control of the flow of information is almost a universal practice of people inside and outside of government who wish to control policy. Control of policy is what governmental and corporate secrecy is mostly about, notwithstanding the plausible rationales of national security and proprietary trade secrets. Openness of information about these relationships means a larger audience, which promotes accountability; this, in turn, means a stronger deterrence to illegal, wasteful, negligent, or unwise decisions. A unique characteristic of the federal Freedom of Information Act is that its enforcement proceeds from citizens and not from government. Remedies or sanctions have to be initiated by citizen petition.

RIGHT OF CHALLENGE AND APPEAL

Standing to challenge or to appeal should be a right of anyone who is exposed to actual or potential injury, or who—as some state environmental laws already provide—stands in a relationship of trust with respect to jeopardized or damaged ecological resources. For decades the judicial assertion of "lack of standing to sue" has driven from the courts, and from the regulatory agencies, consumers, taxpayers, and others who were unable to prove financial damage to themselves. This antiquated and pernicious doctrine—loosened in recent years, but experiencing a comeback under the Burger Court—has arbitrarily shut the majority of our population out of the legal system on many crucial issues.

FREER ACCESS TO THE LEGAL SYSTEM

An associated obstruction to the use of the U.S. legal system by aggrieved parties is the cost of entering that system. While some progress has been made in providing counsel to indigents who are criminally accused, the cost chasm remains for civil suits and for the entire arena of state and federal regulatory, subsidy, and grant agencies. Legal rights mean little without adequate remedies and representation. In our country, this means lawyers and the experts brought together by lawyers. Provision of counsel, the right to collect legal fees from the government if the petitioner prevails, group legal services, and other similar changes would go far toward providing people access to a system that is rapidly becoming a source of decisive inequity.

A LESS SECURE AND
MORE RESPONSIBLE BUREAUCRACY

Power is apt to be more responsibly exercised if it remains insecure. Hence, *insecurity* must be part and parcel of the Civil Service System if it is to be accountable to the citizens it is supposed to serve. The present security of tenure of civil servants, which originated in the merit system, tends to make them irresponsible and unresponsive to the public. One of the most important questions facing our society is how to make bureaucratic systems work efficiently, how to displace them when they are beyond recovery, and how to develop governmental organizations that motivate their members to avoid redundancy and to accept responsibility. Unfortunately, the typical reactions of the public to bureaucracy in the past have been either highly theoretical analyses with little empirical content, or else satire, ridicule, and mass alienation.

Civil servant accountability was the subject of one of our studies entitled *The Spoiled System* to be published by Charterhouse Press. The author, Robert Vaughn, thoroughly analyzed the Civil Service Commission as a regulator of people working in government. He recommended that a process be developed whereby citizens could reach offending government employees with suitable sanctions. Our studies of government agencies persuade us that bureaucracies of any kind —private or public—will not be responsible and responsive unless the people in those bureaucracies are held accountable. They must not be permitted to use the bureaucracy as a buffer or as a means of shifting the focus of responsibility.

This principle can be applied by requiring heads of agencies to spend some time each year at the lower levels—"on the line," so to speak. U.S. presidents should visit their departments and agencies. Company presidents should spend a few days at the factory, plant, or mine, side by side with the employees. Personal contact remains a valid stimulus in achieving perspective, empathy, and reordered priorities—an antidote to parochialism.

SAFEGUARDS AGAINST CORRUPTION

The flow of favors and funds from business to government officials has been increasing in subtlety as well as in volume. The corrupting influence of campaign contributions is all too evident from a perusal of recent news reports and prosecutions. Less evident has been the baleful impact of "deferred bribes." These are the job offers and sinecures communicated by businessmen in various ways to people in government who have something of value to bestow to business (or to withhold). Suggestions for change here are legion; the difficult challenge is how to make reforms that will combine the assurance of judgmental independence by civil servants with a minimum of restriction upon their mobility. Conflict-of-interest legislation can also present difficult technical problems; but these are being alleviated in an increasing number of states by the requirement of disclosure of personal finances by public officials.

Part III

THE DIALOGUE

CHAPTER 5

Diagnosis of the Contemporary Relationship

Dean Williams: I have asked Neil Jacoby to accept the chairmanship of this seminar.

Jacoby: The central issue before us is: What's wrong with the American business-government relationship and how can it be made more productive? A reading of your papers has suggested that we should divide the seminar into three sessions. The first session will be devoted to diagnosis of the relationship. The second will explore the particular topics within the field that deserve prior attention. The third will consider the strategy of implementing whatever program the conferees believe the Norton Simon Commission should undertake.

Let us turn our attention to diagnosis of the contemporary business-government relationship. I'll first call on Daniel Bell for a statement; then I will recognize other individuals in the order in which they indicate a wish to speak.

Bell: I'd like to propose a research inquiry into: Who has power in America? If we are going to develop a fruitful climate for business-government relationships, we should have an accurate sense of where power really lies in American society.

I was puzzled by some of the papers submitted to this seminar, particularly those written by businessmen. The image they convey is that of businessmen being harassed and oppressed by government. Birdzell's paper suggests "guerrilla warfare" between government and business. This is unrealistic. We live in a capitalist society and there is fundamental agreement on its nature. Most people—including academics and liberals—assume that the business community profits most from our society. Government regulation—which we know can be ponderous and heavy-handed—is not aimed at the destruction of the system but at the regulation of particular enterprises or business functions. The public at large believes that businessmen benefit most in this society in terms of income and status. There is no effort to destroy the system.

My paper raised the question: To what extent is business itself responsible for the kind of regulation it gets? I think that to a considerable extent business gets the regulation it deserves. For example, ten years ago, the auto industry was one of the least regulated in the nation, and today it is one of the most regulated. The reason is its own slothfulness in dealing with the problems of safety and air pollution. It could have avoided such regulation if it had been forehanded in anticipating them.

Weidenbaum: There are different kinds of power. If one has in mind ownership of wealth, then the business community is very powerful. If one speaks of decision-making power, then the concern expressed in many papers prepared for this seminar is that more and more of it is passing into the public sector.

Blumenthal: The notion is widespread that the top 100 or 200 business corporations on the *Fortune* list have a very powerful influence upon the vital decisions of American society; but I think that this is incorrect. The groups that really influence public decisions are the milk producers, the cotton textile industry, and other strategically located groups—many consisting of small businesses—that have great power with respect to particular policy decisions. The largest corporations typically do not have such a high degree of influence.

Ramo: I question the assertion that ours is a capitalist economy. It is really a hybrid economy, composed of private enterprises, public enterprises, and mixed enterprises—some profit-motivated and others not. The average voter or consumer who sees a social problem looks to the government rather than to business to come up with a solution. At the same time, paradoxically, he holds a low opinion of government performance.

Public confidence in business has also declined. A Harris poll in 1966 showed that 59 percent of Americans had a high order of confidence in our big business corporations, and the same poll taken recently showed that only 29 percent had a high degree of confidence. To what extent is business responsible for this decline? To what extent does it reflect public misunderstanding?

Weston: It's true that ours is a hybrid economic system. But economic theory offers no answer to the problem of business-government relationships, because that relationship ramifies into the whole social system. We have an essentially capitalist economy linked to a democratic political system in a pluralistic society that is governed by interest groups.

The question: Who has power in America? can be answered, in one way, by looking at the legislation that has been passed, which reflects power that has been exercised. The nature of the whole stream of federal legislation since the early 1930s would appear to be inconsistent with the view that business is the dominant influence in our society. Other interest groups have had dominant influence. Other interest groups have had more of the flow of national resources directed in their favor.

Our nation seems to go through periods of major income reshuffling, when one also sees a revision of popular attitudes toward the roles of business and government. Thus, during the recession of the early 1930s, attitudes toward business turned adverse. Again, during the 1960s, the resource-draining effects of the Vietnam War, launched at the same time as the Great Society programs, implied a lowering of the real incomes of the middle classes. This had an unsettling effect on popular attitudes toward business, government, and other social institutions.

It is in this context that one should assess the performance of the U.S. auto industry. In a period of general discontent and heightened consciousness of externalities, it was obliged to make difficult decisions regarding the tradeoff between safety and freedom from pollution on the one hand, and minimum costs of vehicles on the other. It is not clear that the industry was "slothful."

Meyer: Two points stood out from my reading of the papers of the participants: First, government is not very efficient at delivering goods and services, but business is. Second, business is not effective in identifying social problems and mobilizing corrective action, whereas government is. This led me to ask: How can these two institutions be organized so that each performs its function best?

I have long been struck by the fact that, the longer government operates in a particular area of the business-government relationship, the more it degenerates. Now I understand the reason. Government's true role is identifying problems and mobilizing resources for action. This task is usually completed rather early in a relationship. Thereafter, governmental action can degenerate into unproductive wheel-spinning, while the private sector carries the program to completion.

My conclusions are two: *First,* that government's role is to identify areas where the market mechanism has failed and to motivate business to take corrective action. This will necessarily involve some tensions between the two institutions. It is fallacious to think the relationship will be perfectly cooperative. It is much like the labor-management relationship, in which two adversaries compromise their positions in order to collaborate toward a goal. *Second,* the key to more effective performance by government is to get more turnover in government agencies. We have too often failed to phase out an agency or department after it has completed its job.

Birdzell: I agree that a way should be found to get public institutions to retire when they cease to be useful. This is the primary role of competition in the private sector—to get rid of the unfit. It's a brutal role in practice, and the courts can't stand the sight of it when it is presented in antitrust suits; but it is essential.

With respect to harassment, I think that all persons in high authority—in business, government, the church, or elsewhere—should feel harassed. President Truman said, "If you can't stand the heat, you should get out of the kitchen." The fact that executives feel harassed shows that the system of checks and balances in our pluralistic society is working.

I suggest that the answer to Bell's question, Who has power in America? is "nobody." Power is so diffused that we have difficulty in coping with real social problems. I suspect that public perceptions of the power of business or of government are no more than a secondary datum point. If President Kennedy's staff were inventing a slogan today for a new run for the presidency, instead of, "Getting this country going again," it might well be, "Putting this country back together again."

Referring to Meyer's analogy of the business-government relationship to the labor-management relationship, labor and management in this country have come to understand over the years that they have certain areas of common interest in which they work together. The steel industry is an example. Perhaps this pattern should be an objective of business-government relationships.

Boulding: The business-government relationship should be seen as a rather small subset to the total set of relationships in our society. Most ordinary people do not identify themselves either with "government" or with "business," but with an occupation or a profession. The relations between government and business depend more on the total matrix of the society than upon any interaction between the two institutions. The social dynamics of the United States during the last thirty years have been predominantly internal; external relations are almost peripheral.

I argue that the dynamics of legitimacy dominate all other dynamic factors in our social system, and that they have been strongly influenced by international concerns. The two major structural changes in the American economy over the last half-century have been the decline of agriculture and the rise of the defense industry. Resources released from agriculture have gone into defense—and that is why we all feel no better off. Just as cancer is due to a failure of the defense system of the human body, so one may argue that national defense has become a cancer in American society. The effort to defend almost invariably destroys what you are trying to defend.

We must also consider the legitimacy of our lifestyle. If the world is running out of resources, then the lush lifestyle of the past becomes indecent. It will lose legitimacy.

Meyer: Speaking of structural economic changes, we should not overlook the *private nonprofit* sector of our economy, which is growing rapidly. It includes most of medicine, and much of higher education, some of the insurance industry, the savings and loan industry, and the research and development industry. It is already a big chunk of the economy.

Neal: I'd like to begin with a story about the freshman days of Senator Vandenburg of Michigan. Like most legislators, he wished to introduce bills that would please his constituents. When the tariff issue came up, he looked over the "free list" and found that "beeswax" was on it. He said to himself, "We've got a lot of beekeepers in Michigan and I'll introduce a bill to put a tariff on beeswax which will make them all happy." Whereupon he did—and the heavens fell in upon him! He was besieged with letters from irate constituents. So he went to Senator Watson, then the counselling dean of the Senate, and asked his advice. Senator Watson said, "Well, have you been in a Catholic church and seen those little burning candles? They have a heavy component of beeswax. When you get your beekeepers as well organized as the Catholics are, your bill may have a chance!"

When we discuss power in society, one must distinguish between the power-to-start and the power-to-stop. One structural change needed in our society is a reduction in the power-to-stop. The nation lacks power plants; it lacks deep-water ports capable of serving supertankers; and it lacks oil from the continental shelves—all because of the power-to-stop wielded by environmental groups and governmental agencies. Business has great difficulty in getting positive action from government to offset the veto power exercised by well-established groups all over the nation, such as the Sierra Club.

Another difficulty is that the performance standards of business and government differ. Business seeks profit and therefore emphasizes improved productivity. Government seeks to satisfy constituents, and has long neglected productivity in its operations. Improved productivity should also become a performance standard in government.

Noll: The observations that have been made about the pluralism of American society, and that neither business nor any other group controls it, are true; but they are not really relevant. Our political process should be characterized as one of *vote magnification*. Political action does *not* represent an equally weighted aggregation of everyone's preferences, because the influences of some voters is magnified and that of others is reduced. Some persons are better organized than others; some are more eloquent than others; some have dollars to influence elections and legislation while others do not. Also, the political "industry" is one of very imperfect competition with high barriers to entry.

For example, there is about a $2 million barrier to becoming a candidate for U.S. senator from California.

This kind of political system may produce tolerably satisfactory results, so long as society's goal is increased production and material welfare. But the system can break down in an affluent society, if the social goal is an improved quality of life with less pollution, congestion, and noise, and better interpersonal relations. Today's society takes collective action to impose institutional restraints upon the production system. As our society gets richer and its goals become more complex, these conflicts will become more difficult to resolve. It is utopian to think we can have a cooperative relationship between business and government that is free of conflicts.

The relevant question is: How can we build institutions that are effective in implementing our society's *present* set of preferences? The main flaw in present governmental institutions, such as the regulatory agencies, is that they were designed a long time ago to solve different problems, and they are incredibly ineffective in solving contemporary problems. If this seminar is to do something useful, it should devise institutional innovations for satisfying the new value system of American society.

Bell: I would like to reiterate my question: Who has power in America? because it needs an answer before one can deal with structural changes in society. Usually, the question of power does not come up so long as people are tolerably satisfied with the existing state of affairs. In the United States, the people who have power are those who have dominant interests and concerns and the ability to manifest them.

We should also ask the question: Why does government enter particular areas? It does so when there is an evident sense of failure —when something is wrong. The current energy problem is a prime example. When there are failures, there is a rush of concern. Government passes laws and tries to regulate. The fundamental problem is to define the areas of failure, and to decide how government *should* respond.

Too often, government responds with overkill, its response becomes rigid, and businessmen feel that sense of harassment to which Birdzell referred. For example, the Interstate Commerce Act of 1887 was a proper response of government to the excessive economic power of the railroads, which they were abusing. Later, the ICC became rigid and counterproductive, after the railroads lost their monopoly on surface transportation.

Why do failures occur? To some extent they are due to shifts in basic societal preferences. Sometimes they are attributable to the unresponsiveness of business to popular demands. There may be many reasons. But, there have been large failures of the economic system, and they have provoked governmental regulation as a response.

Ramo: The basic issue before us is not "who has power," because we all know that power is widely diffused. The basic issue is how to define the respective roles of government and business in our society.

In our hybrid society, there are bound to be failures of the market system, and this is not disastrous. Take the auto industry as an example. The mission of an automobile manufacturer is to try to figure out what kind of auto the public will buy, and to supply that presumed demand. It is *not* to decide the amount of safety that society at large desires, or the emissions of pollutants it will tolerate. This is the mission of government. If one auto maker presumed to decide these matters for the nation, and then had to charge more for his vehicles, and other auto makers did not do so, the first company would suffer a loss. Only government can set the standards that society wants, and can enforce them on all firms in the auto industry. Thus the role of the profit-seeking enterprise is limited.

Take the case of TRW, Inc., which makes automotive parts. Our company decided years ago that the production of foreign cars would rise faster than the output of American cars. It also concluded that the U.S. demand for small cars would increase greatly. So, in response to the profit motive, it established automotive parts factories in many foreign countries and expanded its facilities for making parts for small cars. Fortunately, the company correctly anticipated changes in market demand and profited accordingly. But it might have been wrong, and then suffered a loss.

The point is that government must set the standards and rules for the market; businesses then compete within this framework for the patronage of the public.

Jacoby: I'd like to call on those participants who have not yet expressed themselves: First, Ralph Nader.

Nader: The business-government relationship can be discussed at many levels of abstraction. I'd like to take the *procedural* approach. We can discuss at least eight categories of relationships: taxation, regulation, subsidies and loans, contracts, grants, licenses and leases, promotional standards, and regulation of the claimant process (lobbying, conflicts of interest, rights of appeal, etc.). Government has a great deal to give, and also a great deal to withhold. Most of the political conflict in Washington has been over the scope and pace of providing for, or withholding from, various interest groups, including business. Hence, power *is* the problem, procedurally as well as substantively.

One basic procedural issue is control of the *stream of information.* Whoever controls the flow of information has gone a long way toward controlling the flow of public policy. The Freedom of Information Act of 1967 gave citizens the right to challenge governmental secrecy in the courts; but it exempted intra-agency materials, proprietary data, and national security data. The federal agencies have automatically withheld from the public information labelled by businesses as "proprietary" or "trade secret," without justifying such action. This prevents the policymaking process in Washington from being opened up to more diverse points of view. Even information provided by companies to their trade associations has been claimed to be a "trade secret." Lack of availability of proprietary and national security data has done much to centralize control over policymaking in Washington. The Freedom of Information Act is not enforced by government—only by citizens.

Another procedural issue concerns *standing to sue, to challenge, or to appeal from governmental actions or inactions.* Lack of this privilege has long been a prime barrier to use of the legal system by consumers and by taxpayers. In recent years, this obstacle has been diminished to some degree; but the present U.S. Supreme Court appears to be returning to a more restrictive definition of "standing to sue."

A third procedural matter is the *cost of entering the legal system.* Some progress has been made in providing counsel at public expense to indigent persons accused of crimes or misdemeanors. Yet there cannot be meaningful legal rights without adequate remedies and representation for all citizens. For instance, a person who buys an auto from General Motors that turns out to be a "lemon" has the right to sue General Motors; but this may mean little if he cannot afford the costs of adequate representation in the courts. Provision of counsel at public expense, the right to collect legal fees from the government if the petitioner prevails, and group legal services are proposals that merit close attention. The power of corporate sellers is apt to be more responsive if it remains insecure—as a result of full access of buyers to the courts.

An important way to improve business-government relationships is to reform the civil service system. While it emerged as a response to the evils of the spoils system, presumably replacing service to the party with technical merit as a criterion for appointment, it has *not* resulted in accountability outward to the public that the system is supposed to serve. Its accountability is upward—not outward.

The quickest way to lose a government job is to *do* the job of serving the public. A pervasive characteristic of Washington bureaucracy is that almost nothing a bureaucrat does, or does not do, will get him fired, demoted, or fined, except outright bribery—or offending his political superiors. There are chronicles of twenty-year refusals to enforce regulatory laws, of prolonged absences of civil servants from their jobs, of chronic suppression of information. Yet one searches in vain for evidence that any penalties have been imposed for such behavior.

An inquiry might well be organized into ways of making the civil service bureaucracy accountable to the people. Robert Vaughn of The

Center for the Study of Responsive Law has written a study of the civil service system, *The Spoiled System,* which contains two recommendations. One is that citizens be enabled to call offending governmental employees to account. Another is that measures be taken to *fix* personal accountability for actions—or inactions. One of the self-protective devices of bureaucracy is to institutionalize the diffusion of responsibility in such ways that it cannot be focused upon any individual. Personal accountability to the public is evaded. This must be corrected.

Finally, steps should be taken to *stem the flow of favors and funds from business to government officials.* The corrupting influence of campaign contributions needs no elaboration these days. Less evident has been the baleful impact of a phenomenon that can be called the "deferred bribe." This occurs when government officials are led to believe that they will find attractive positions in business or trade associations after they leave government service. Well over two thirds of the officials who left positions in the Federal Communications Commission and the Interstate Commerce Commission during the last few decades are now consulting or working for the industries they formerly regulated. The challenge is to bring about reforms that will prevent conflicts of interest without impairing occupational mobility unduly.

Weidenbaum: I agree with Nader that barriers to the flow of information impede the development of good business-government relations, and that sometimes government as well as business is at fault. When I was studying the impact of defense activity on the Seattle economy, the Departments of Commerce and Labor refused to provide data on Boeing's employment on the grounds that it was proprietary information; but Boeing itself provided the data!

Birdzell: Government certainly needs better information from the private sector in order to formulate effective monetary-fiscal policies. For example, labor unions have unjustifiably opposed the decomposition of figures on total unemployment, although they are needed to ascertain how much unemployment can be attacked by monetary-fiscal policy and how much by other means. Modern corporations sooner or later are going to have to live in glass houses. I think that if they showed everything they had, people would be greatly disappointed to discover that there isn't anything very interesting there!

Much business opposition to disclosure of more information arises from a feeling that the information will be mishandled by the receiver. The facts that are disclosed must always be fitted into some framework of analysis. Who will do this? The broadcaster often feels that nobody has a receiver capable of "making music" out of what he transmits.

Nader's comments reminded me of Carl Kaysen's observation, in his Holmes Lectures at Harvard some years ago, that the great difference between business and government is that business is organized to get something done, while government's actions are severely constrained by the requirement of doing justice—of being fair. He concluded that this was a severe restriction upon the ability of government to solve major social problems.

Nader's proposition that procedure is important is music to the ears of anyone trained in the common law. (In the first year of law school I learned that "substance arises in the interstices of procedure.") However, it is possible that government will become so preoccupied with doing justice through procedural means that its ability to do anything else will be sharply limited. One can, in other words, achieve *undue* process of law. In the long run, a government that is focused upon due process of law is going to be a government with a very restricted role in society.

Jacoby: Is effective competition inconsistent with complete and full disclosure of all data and plans by business firms?

Birdzell: This can be a problem. If one's competitors fully disclosed all costs, sales volumes, and profits by product line, and all their plans for the future, one might decide to go out of business!

Ramo: I cannot conceive of any degree of disclosure that would not be satisfactory, provided that it applied to *all* competitors. Even if we all knew what our competitors were doing, there would still be adequate scope for competitive effort.

Fitzhugh: When we discuss the question: Who has power? we should not overlook the labor unions and the media. With respect to procedural issues, our society should follow a course of moderation. If everyone can bring an action in court any time he feels like it, nothing will ever get done.

A basic reason for contemporary discontent is that people have been led to expect the millennium from government, and when it fails to deliver, they get upset. The Great Society is a case in point. Perhaps the best thing the Norton Simon Commission could do would be to educate the public to lower its expectations.

Linowitz: I think that business as well as government has helped in recent years to *raise* popular expectations.

Fitzhugh: I didn't mean to exonerate business!

Bell: Public discontent is really due to something I call the Jouvenel effect. Bertrand de Jouvenel observed that peoples' satisfactions do not rise proportionately to their real incomes. If a person's income doubles, he expects to live twice as well; but he cannot do so because other people's incomes have also risen; they are generating more externalities, and he is competing with them for the available supply of amenities. This effect is a deep structural characteristic of modern society, and not merely a matter of overselling people.

Steiner: I'd like to add another dimension to this discussion. A major problem in our society is identifying problems that lie ahead. Our mechanisms for identification are terribly defective, and our ability to deal with the problems we do identify is even worse. The energy crisis is an example. As our society becomes more complex, its problems are going to become more difficult. The urgency of planning is increasing.

I agree with Nader's observations about bureaucracy. And I think Meyer's proposal is astute—that we would get better performance out of government agencies if they had a terminal date on their existence. My own experience in government during World War II and the Korean conflict taught me that the quality of management and the speed of decision making is infinitely better in an action-laden agency dealing with a crisis and having a terminal date on its existence than in an old-line government bureau.

Heyns: Aren't your two propositions contradictory? Only if our government continues to be faced with unanticipated crises as a result of lack of planning will it continue to have impromptu agencies that will be highly effective and disappear! *(Laughter)*

Steiner: Not necessarily. Government can and should have effective mechanisms for looking ahead and identifying problems; it should *also* establish temporary agencies for coping with them.

Noll: Agencies of short duration are not applicable to *all* that government should do. There are many social problems—state and local as well as national and international—that need *continual* monitoring. Environmental protection, for example, will require a substantial amount of governmental control and surveillance in perpetuity. But we don't want the Environmental Protection Agency to become another ICC.

Meyer: One can exaggerate the need for *continuous* monitoring of the environment. To get public behavior up to standard, there will have to be a bureaucracy at first. But after industry and consumers have made the necessary investments and become accustomed to the new standards, environmental protection can become a fairly automatic process. The need for a big bureaucracy will decline substantially, but history teaches that the size of the bureaucracy will not!

Blumenthal: It is important to recruit first-rate personnel into government to work on all social problems. We *should* expect a higher level of efficiency in government, a more uniform system of justice, and a better capability to plan. But government contains relatively few people of great excellence, and very many of mediocre ability. This results from the mode of operation of the Civil Service Commission, its methods of recruitment, and lack of adequate incentives for superior performance, including pay scales. The pay structure of government is too compressed at the top. It is unrealistic to expect government officials to be very good in anticipating future problems and laying plans to resolve them. Business doesn't do a very good job of this either.

Ramo: Advancing technology has an important bearing upon the business-government relationship. Name any problem you wish, whether it is international economic warfare, consumerism, control of inflation, race relations, urbanization, or urban design, and you will find that technological progress is the driving force behind change and is a great creator of crises.

Some of the more important social tasks ahead cannot be performed by simple extensions of free-market private enterprise. They call for so many billions of dollars, such high risks, and such long-deferred returns that not even the largest corporation can undertake them. I refer to the problems of energy supply, of air transportation, of communications systems, or of mass urban transportation. One cannot design a good urban transportation system until he knows how the city should be designed. These new problems require government involvement to a degree, and in a manner, that is closer to its role in the building of nuclear weaponry or landing a man on the moon, than it is to its role in regard to the typical services and products that come out of the classical enterprise system. New kinds of business-government relationships will be needed to cope with the social problems that arise from technological change.

Meyer: While I agree with some of your statements, I think it's easy to overgeneralize. Take urban transportation: Part of this problem is that government has artificially scaled it up, thus preventing new technology from being effective. For example, cities suppressed jitneys by their franchising policies. Some of the difficulties people in ghettos have in getting to industrial jobs could be surmounted by jitneys or car pools. Also, cities need new express bus services running from high-density suburbs or housing clusters into central-city offices. But vested interests and franchising procedures suppress them. In short, the available new transport technologies have been artificially kept on a large scale, which makes for far too much interaction between government and business.

Ramo: You are helping to make my point. I do not argue that we should necessarily adopt large-scale transportation technology. I do assert that today we lack communication between government and the private sector, and we lack the joint decision-making structures to select and implement the *optimum* technology of transportation.

Meyer: I dislike being cynical, but my observation of urban transportation leads me to state a basic rule: The most expensive solution will be favored by public officials. This is so for a variety of reasons, not the least of which may often be a vested interest in awarding large contracts.

Heyns: So far we have been discussing the regulatory function of government, and how it deals with defects in the private sector. We should also discuss the other functions of government, which include meeting the social goals of health, education, welfare, employment, etc.

Jacoby: I have some difficulty reconciling Meyer's call for small-scale solutions to urban transportation with the emphasis he puts in his paper on the need for mixed public-private enterprises.

Meyer: I did *not advocate* mixed public-private enterprises; I was merely observing an historical trend toward them. They can be better than pure government organizations for many purposes. We should follow the old maxim of Occam's razor: Where there are several solutions to a problem, it is best to choose the simplest! For example, if there is a problem of redistributing income among different income classes in society, we are better off to use the direct income transfer devices available in the fiscal structure than to use differential price controls, housing programs, etc. These latter devices mix extraneous objectives up with income redistribution; and they unnecessarily complicate business-government relationships.

Nader: Referring back to Fitzhugh's call for a lower level of public expectations, it should be pointed out that life insurance companies have succeeded in doing this—they have reduced people's expectations of longer life. They have persuaded people to take into account the contingency of accidents and bad health by buying life, accident, and health insurance. (And, parenthetically, the mutual life insurance company is theoretically a highly democratic type of organization, but in practice the policyholders don't exercise their rights, and they leave the managements free to act as they see fit.)

We must remember that government is the repository of the gap between the potential benefits the private sector can provide consumers and its actual performance. A major public tension today arises from the high expectations that people hold about technological abundance and the actual scarcities that exist.

Many technological advances are stalled, not by government agencies, but by business corporations committed to old technologies. For example, AT&T's investments in cable communications are challenged by communication satellites. And cable television is a challenge to the electronic networks. The potential technological abundance of solar energy is a challenge to now-scarce fossil fuels. Technological progress raises public expectations, and if the economic system is not ready to translate them into realities, the result is public cynicism and alienation.

How can this problem be overcome? The traditional prescriptions are antitrust enforcement and reform of the patent laws. Venture capital is also needed, but the great sources of capital—banks and insurance companies—prefer to serve established customers. Thus, the energy industry is now contemplating the investment of hundreds of billions of dollars in the recovery of oil from shale, but plans virtually no investment in solar energy.

Jacoby: In concluding this morning's session, I ask you to give thought to two issues on the agenda that have not yet been discussed. One is the culpability of business for a less-than-satisfactory relationship with government. We have criticized government on many grounds, but so far few adverse remarks have been made about the performance of business. A second issue is what, if anything, Americans can learn about the business-government relationship in other industrialized nations that might merit emulation here.

This afternoon we will try to focus discussion on remedies for the problems we have so precisely diagnosed! *(Laughter)*

CHAPTER 6

Setting Priorities for Education and Research

Jacoby: Let us direct our discussion to those issues in the American business-government relationship that merit special study or education: What are the main gaps in our knowledge of the relationship? What are the key areas of ignorance or misunderstanding that need illumination? What priorities should be assigned to particular topics?

We will follow a freewheeling format, and whoever is under the strongest impulse may speak first!

Weidenbaum: I think the major gap in our professional knowledge and in public understanding concerns the impact of government upon the entrepreneurial character of the business enterprise. We should known more about what happens to the behavior of the firm as government increasingly involves itself in what were formerly internal decisions of management. What is government regulation costing society in attenuation of business risk-bearing and in loss of productivity?

Meyer: I agree that this is an area of ignorance. But the social costs of some regulatory programs are sometimes overestimated because the private sector adapts to them by finding lower cost solutions, not at first known or identified. Environmental regulation is an outstanding example.

Williams: At meetings of boards of directors I have heard managements complain about the costs of minority employment programs, and other governmental regulations. Is there a positive correlation between levels of complaint and levels of cost?

Weidenbaum: What got me started was an order of the Consumer Product Safety Commission in St. Louis. It ordered the dumping of thousands of gallons of solvent intended for washing the windshields of autos, because the label lacked the warning: "Cannot be made non-poisonous." They could have ordered the printing of new labels instead, but they weren't concerned about costs. The same Commission is now proposing to recall several million electric frying pans, although there has not been a single case reported of hazard to consumers. Its idea seems to be "consumer safety at any cost."

Steiner: Ignorance of the effects of governmental regulation of business encompasses benefits as well as costs. We have neglected benefit-cost analysis of governmental programs. For example, clean air and clean water standards have generally been based upon guesswork and emotion, rather than upon careful appraisal of the costs and benefits of alternative standards.

Jacoby: Your comment suggests that any governmental agency proposing a new regulation or program might well be *required* to make a benefit-cost analysis, demonstrating a net social benefit from its action. Builders and developers must now produce a favorable environmental impact report before they can go ahead with a new project.

Williams: How can this lack of concern about the costs of governmental regulation be explained?

Weidenbaum: By public ignorance of the role of costs, prices, and profits in our economic system.

Heyns: This discussion is oversimplified. Officials required to set earthquake-resistant standards for constructing buildings, or labelling standards for drugs, are living in a social environment which is intolerant of taking *any* risk. They are thinking of their accountability to the public for what might happen.

Weidenbaum: The system is biased toward excessively high standards. Whenever the regulator says, "You must make it safer," he is protected. If he says, "Well, it's safe enough," he *may* catch hell!

Neal: Almost all governmental programs are adopted without a thorough exploration of alternative means of achieving the end being sought. The Committee for Economic Development has recently studied alternative programs to achieve EPA water quality standards. As a result, we are recommending that the present program be scrapped, both because it is inefficient and also because the zero effluent standard for 1985 is simply unachievable at anything less than an astronomical cost.

Heyns: I agree that the public should know what it will cost to meet environmental standards. What I am suggesting is that large uncertainties are inherent in the process of setting standards, and public officials will seek to avoid risks by setting high standards. For example, new drugs are usually tested on animals, and their effects on humans are less certain.

Weidenbaum: The Department of Labor estimates that it would cost the auto industry roughly $1 billion to install the safety harness buzzer systems in the 1974 cars. Were the social payoffs from this massive investment calculated in advance? [Note: Congress abolished this requirement late in 1974.]

Blumenthal: Attention to benefits and costs *was* given to the safety harness buzzer system, and also to air bags as one alternative. However, the basic proposition that benefit-cost ratios should be computed for all alternative means of attaining any of the goals set by our government is very important.

Williams: Can reliable benefit-cost analysis be made for many programs? Why isn't more of it being done?

Neal: Most government agencies are not motivated, or equipped, to make such analyses. Also, experiments are required, and governments are bad at conducting them—witness the Model Cities Program.

Boulding: There are two obstacles to benefit-cost analysis. One is that the people who pay the costs usually are not those who get the benefits, and the success of any political process depends upon there being an optimal degree of ignorance—the people who are adversely affected must not know, or else they will object and nothing will be done.

The other obstacle is the firm conviction in our society that random events should be "acts of God," not under human control. We refuse to put a price on human life—it raises an issue of political ethics of enormous magnitude. Who, for example, would *plan* the death of 60,000 Americans a year on the highways? A dispassionate benefit-cost analysis would conclude that the number of medical schools should be cut in half and medical research should be prohibited—their marginal productivity is negative! The medical profession is now mainly concerned with keeping alive old people who ought to be dead.

Jacoby: In this connection, Professor Sam Peltzman of the UCLA faculty studied the effects of the 1962 Amendments to the Federal Food and Drug Act, which required lengthy testing of new drugs before they could be put on the market. His well-documented conclusion is that far more people suffered illness and death from the delay in the availability of new drugs than had suffered ill effects from the early availability of untested drugs. The new testing program is thus counterproductive.

Ramo: Let me put a question about public policy to deal with the energy crisis: Suppose you are the President of the United States with power to make the necessary decisions and with the popular support to put them into effect. One course is to let competitive market forces work out a solution. Energy prices will rise, energy consumption will be curtailed, returns on energy investment will go up, and private enterprises will in time bring forth larger domestic supplies of energy. A second course is for the government to curtail consumption by various means, to engage in research on new energy sources, and to engage in energy production. The future business-government relationship in dealing with energy is determined by which course is followed. What do we do? How do we decide the matter?

Bell: You cannot decide solely on a basis of which course is the most *efficient*. It is necessary to take into account the degree of *fairness* of each course, and how it affects different groups in society. For example, rationing gasoline by price may be efficient; but it will "iron out" those who cannot afford one dollar per gallon gasoline; they will want ration coupons to buy at a lower price.

Meyer: I have already argued that it is wrong to mix up income redistribution with regulation. Better to avoid a rationing system, and to take care of the needy by a negative income tax or another kind of transfer payment.

Bell: You may be right in theory, but not in terms of practical politics. It is important that people believe the system is "fair."

Meyer: We should educate the people about all of the possibilities.

Bell: I believe that governmental intervention is inevitable in dealing with every social issue. The real question is how to minimize detailed regulation, which becomes heavy-handed and bureaucratic. For example, taxation of water pollution can be a fiscal incentive for curbing pollution. But if the business community fights such a tax, which utilizes market forces, it probably will find itself obliged to meet tough antipollution standards that do *not* use market forces.

Meyer: I am sympathetic to your last point. However, one should not oversimplify. The most efficient way to abate water pollution may be to make a systems analysis on the relevant water basin, and to regulate effluents where they occur, rather than to tax polluters.

Rice: It is necessary to look at the use to be made of each river basin, and to build a regulatory scheme around it.

Linowitz: I agree with Bell that business should not simply call for reliance on market forces in meeting the energy problem, without showing concern for the person who cannot afford very high prices for energy. That attitude is responsible for much public disrespect for business as an institution.

Neal: That is true. Businesses have been the chief polluters of our lakes and streams. Business did not have well-conceived and tested plans for coping with water pollution. So it got what it deserved—ill-fitting and unrealistic legislation. A socially sensitive and responsive business will see social problems coming down the road, and will devote resources to finding a way to deal with them. Businessmen should take leadership; they should be out ahead of the politicians.

Weidenbaum: This gets to the heart of the matter. The great fault of business has been a failure to anticipate social problems and to propose rational solutions to the government—leading to "too much, too late" action by government. Maybe this is due to the fact that executives in business get the top job only about five years before their retirement. So they fend off social problems, hoping to leave them to their successors.

Nader: I used to believe this until I studied the Ford Motor Company's record on auto safety. Ford's chairman was then about fifty-two and its president was about forty-eight years old.

Meyer: Maybe Ford felt it could not do much by itself. The initiative had to come from General Motors, which had the largest share of the auto market. We should remember that Ford had an earlier bad experience with a "safe automobile" campaign.

Nader: Let me correct that widely accepted myth. Ford decided to emphasize safety in marketing its 1956 models, and the safety features were selling very well. Later, Ford changed the theme of its advertising to style and power not because "safety doesn't sell," but because Ford had broken the advertising code of the auto industry, which prohibited the kind of competitive advertising that said: "Ford is safer than Chevrolet." Safety was *not* an adverse factor in Ford sales.

Meyer: I am merely seeking an answer to the question: Why business firms, which often have more information than anyone else about efficient solutions to social problems, fail to come to grips with them *ahead* of the public pressure for solutions?

Nader: I found that Ford waits to follow General Motors—it has a follow-the-leader syndrome. GM's power stems from the fact that the rest of the auto industry accepted its merchandising strategy of emphasizing *style* in order to foster an abnormally high rate of sales of new cars. GM was the first auto maker to employ a fulltime stylist; and it has remained first in this field.

Williams: The general question is how the structure of an industry affects its willingness and ability to respond to public pressures.

Meyer: That is the basic question, and we should not generalize from one or two cases.

Linowitz: Firms with a vested interest in a profitable product are loath to change it or to replace it with a new product. There would be no Xerox today if IBM or RCA or Kodak had acquired the xerography process, which was offered to them. Because they were making good profits with their existing products, they turned it down.

Meyer: If General Motors had *known* that the public would demand auto safety, emission controls, and small cars, would its behavior have been different?

Blumenthal: I think the concentrated structure of the industry explains a lot. Ford discontinued its emphasis on safety, even though it was gaining a larger share of the market, because it feared reprisal by General Motors the next year.

Jacoby: So far, we have been discussing only two of the twenty topics on our agenda—reforming governmental regulation of business, and regulation by market forces versus public commissions. We should move on to other topics.

Bell: A very crucial problem is: How does business reform government? The government of our country is highly fragmented and seems to be responsive only to crises. As my colleague Samuel Huntington said: "We have the most modern economy in the world in a Tudor polity." We have an antiquated structure of townships, counties, mosquito abatement districts, and so on. Our governmental structure is in disarray and involves a great waste of tax money. The Committee for Economic Development exposed this condition a few years ago in its admirable brochures, *Modernizing Local Government* and *Modernizing State Government*. The issues are even more crucial today.

Neal: Recently, George Steiner of UCLA, in cooperation with us in CED, surveyed the socially-oriented activities of several hundred large companies, and found that practically none was doing anything about reforming the structure of local government. Yet political fragmentation threatens to fragment our national *market*, which is a key to the high productivity of the U.S. economy. Regulation of business has been proliferating at the local government level. For example, it is legally impossible today to make a child's toy that will satisfy the regulations of all governments of the nation. Suppose this became true of television sets? Of automobiles?

Weidenbaum: Business should deal with this problem through objective studies by universities and independent research institutions.

Linowitz: Business is providing leadership in many cities around the country through urban coalitions, which are studying this problem, along with many others.

Williams: Business may fear to take on this problem because its efforts may appear to be self-serving; and also because they could backfire.

Noll: While I agree that the structure of local government should be rationalized, there is a good reason why people like to deal with small governmental units. People can influence the decisions of local governments, whereas a large unit may be unresponsive to local needs.

Bell: We should not go to extremes. We should have governments whose jurisdictions are small enough to be socially responsive, and yet large enough to be efficient.

Noll: National markets are certainly needed to achieve economies of scale. However, if production of a commodity generates external costs in particular areas, local government action is needed to internalize them—if our government is to be responsive to societal needs.

Ramo: The question put to us was: What is business doing to improve the organization of government? Speaking for my own company, TRW, Inc., we try to be socially aware and responsive, but we are *not* equipped to decide how government should be organized. We do not think it is our job to decide such questions. We lack expertise in that field. If we involved our personnel deeply in such issues, we might fail to make good products profitably, which *is* our job. The political system has the task of weighing social values. We respond to the profit motive and to market opportunities.

Bell: You do yourself a disservice by saying that you work for profits. You need profits to survive, but you really work for the pleasure of technological achievement. The distinction is subtle but important.

Ramo: I'll accept that, but it does not change our activities.

Bell: It *does* change them, by giving you a responsibility to maintain a vibrant and exciting environment in your company so that people will continue to want to work there.

Linowitz: Obviously, there is a limit to which any company can devote its resources to social purposes without going bankrupt. Yet one can make a persuasive argument for much corporate social involvement that is beneficial to the company.

Jacoby: Are you opposed to corporate philanthropy in the sense of spending money without any quid pro quo?

Linowitz: I am saying that there are many types of corporate gifts for which there is a quid pro quo. For example, in the early 1960s, Xerox undertook to finance four national television programs about the United Nations. The company spent $4 million on these programs, which were without commercial messages apart from "Xerox is proud to present" and "Xerox has presented" at the beginning and at the end. We pioneered. The response was tremendous. We received thousands of letters. People from all over the world came to work for the company. It was a great investment.

Neal: Does there always have to be a quid pro quo for corporate gifts? Can a gift be justified in the broad context of helping to create a healthy country in which to do business?

Linowitz: It is not necessary to have a specific quid pro quo. But many types of corporate gifts have them. In the Xerox example, we reasoned that the company was entering foreign areas, and it wanted to be known as an international firm. The company would benefit from a world at peace, and it was good corporate policy to tell people about the United Nations.

Nader: Historically, American corporations have tried to avoid being evaluated in political terms. This accounts for their reluctance to engage in governmental reform and political activity. The more they are evaluated politically by the public, the less control they have over their enterprise. There has been a movement to broaden the standards of evaluation of corporate behavior—including treatment of employees, of the environment, and so on—and this puts corporations under pressure to broaden their constituencies. They prefer to be evaluated on narrow profit-and-loss standards, as Professor Milton Friedman advocated.

The basic question is whether corporations can afford any more to hold this viewpoint. The basic question is whether rioting cities destroy markets. Decaying neighborhoods are bad for business. Business firms are inescapably involved in politics. But they want to avoid politicization beyond their control.

Meyer: I have been perplexed by the many apparent failures of businesses to anticipate their own future problems, which often entail costly overreactions from the public sector.

Neal: Often, it isn't a matter of *doing* something to reform government but of *stopping* government from doing things. I recall an oil company lobbyist who was asked his opinion of the CED recommendation that state legislators should be paid more. He replied: "My job is to get the legislation passed that we need and to stop the legislation we don't want. If legislators are poor, hungry or even barefooted, I can do my job a lot better."

Birdzell: My answer to Meyer's perplexity is that corporations face the task of foreseeing trends and adjusting to them. There are instances where trends are not detected and adjustments are unrecorded. My guess is that business does very well, overall, in its forecasting and adjustment, in comparison with the abilities of governments to forecast economic conditions and to adjust the relevant monetary and fiscal variables. But if business misses, even 2 percent of the time, its errors are highly visible to the public.

Meyer: You are saying that only business's failures are noted; not its successes. What then, *are* the institutional failings of business in its relationships to government?

Weidenbaum: One is a lamentable lack of understanding of government by business executives. It is important to raise the level of understanding.

Jacoby: Is the businessman's understanding of government less profound than the bureaucrat's understanding of business? The answer will determine *where* education is most needed.

Noll: The effort to identify culprits is rather fruitless. We all have different perceptions of the world and respond differently to our environment and the incentives it contains. The essence of the matter is *institutions* rather than people. The world needs institutions in which rather ignorant people can operate productively. We will never educate people enough to know what social policy should be on every issue.

Weidenbaum: As one who has suffered through both a school of business administration and a school of public administration, I believe it is feasible to give the next generation of business executives an understanding of government, and vice versa.

Blumenthal: Another deficiency of businessmen is failing to understand the need for, and the potentiality of, government. Many look on government as an unavoidable evil, just as they feel intuitively that labor unions are bad.

Bell: In our hybrid economy, it is more realistic to say that there are managers of government bureaus and managers of business enterprises. Most people who think of themselves as "businessmen" are not entrepreneurs in the old-fashioned sense; they are managers. It is symptomatic of the new concept that you have a Graduate School of Management at UCLA instead of a Graduate School of Business. Today we have executives of political institutions and executives of economic institutions.

Noll: People low down in the hierarchy of any institution (e.g., the janitor in a university) may not identify with it or understand it. People at the top of the hierarchical levels move back and forth between academia, government, and business.

Bell: In sociology, "status" means the kind of work one does while "situs" means where you work. Situs is important to people as well as status.

Fitzhugh: One of the hang-ups of businessmen is that they are so involved with the problems of meeting next quarter's profit target that they lack time to consider the long-term future. I would fault businessmen for too short-term a perspective in making decisions. If businessmen thought in terms of long-term profits, they would become socially more involved.

Neal: It is surprising that in both business and government, there is not a practice of recording social contributions each year in a Social Report. We want businesses to be fair to their employees, to produce safe products, to label products more accurately, and so on. But there is no requirement to report their behavior to the public, although they are required to report financial results to the public. We should be able to identify social actions that businesses could measure and report.

Fitzhugh: Some companies are doing it now.

Williams: How do we determine *what* social actions are important to the public? And how can we assure that business and government actions will serve the long-term social welfare, when most top managers in business and most public officials have a tenure of five years or less?

Fitzhugh: Both businessmen and government officials should change their way of thinking. Businessmen who complain that politicians can't see beyond the next election, often can't see beyond their annual financial statement! Both must train themselves to *think long*.

Steiner: The CED and this School surveyed large corporations on the subject of the social audit and got responses from 285 companies. Fifty percent replied that they thought the social audit would become mandatory in the future. Seventy-six percent stated that the idea was acceptable to them as businessmen. Many elaborated reasons why they thought it was a good idea.

Nader: Let's discuss what a Social Report should include. I'd settle if corporations just obeyed the law! *(Laughter)* A corporate crime wave has been underway for a long time, and part of it has begun to surface. It is a crime wave that involves violations of regulations; that forces derivative agencies in the business world to commit the crime as a proxy for the principal; that gets laws passed that exempt business from what would otherwise be civil or criminal violations. *The Wall Street Journal* contains references to an almost geometric upsurge of business violations. The business system should be evaluated by its voluntary abstention from violations of law.

These violations include consumer fraud, environmental pollution, job safety and occupational disease hazards, usury, property tax assessments, financing of political campaigns, securities issuance, sales taxation, lobbying, and weights and measures. A three-strand inquiry is needed: (1) What is the pattern of violation of existing laws? (2) What is the derivative violation by proxy? (3) To what extent are violations avoided by getting special interest privileges from legislatures on one or another pretext?

The preponderance of law enforcement resources is spent on street crime. Little is focused upon business and white-collar crime, such as antitrust violations. The Department of Justice lacks the staff to root out price fixing—not by big companies but by plumbers and electricians. The definition of violence in our country heavily adheres to traditional street crimes, such as burglaries, rapes, and homicides.

But increasingly violence is coming from technology—unsafe products, pesticides in foods, water pollution, and the rest. The law has never come down hard on it because it proceeds from industrial activity that is mainly beneficial to society. Someday, however, it may be thought as serious a crime to pollute a river as to loot a supermarket. (Some primitive tribes penalize pollution of the village water supply more heavily than rape.) We should closely assess noncompliance with, or violation of, laws by business.

Jacoby: Granted that there has been a marked rise in business crime, is this not part of a more general social malaise?

Nader: To use an organic analogy, a society rots from the head down, like a fish. The revelation of law violations by political and business leaders tends to provide a rationalization for petty shoplifters and burglars.

Wiedenbaum: Nader cites *The Wall Street Journal* as a source of information on business crime. I also receive many labor publications; but I cannot recall any containing reports of union violations of law.

Nader: We are discussing business here. I could spend hours describing union violations of law, including the looting of pension funds, the taking of bribes, and so on. But if business looks on itself as a leader and a pacesetter in society, its crime is more serious. Labor union leaders tend to emulate their business counterparts.

Bell: I think Nader is right, but he may exaggerate somewhat. My sense of what has been happening is that what was previously immorality has become illegality. Water pollution is an example.

Nader: I do not condemn business for actions it took legally many years ago which are now illegal. My focus is on *current* noncompliance with *existing* law. The 1899 Anti-Refuse Act, which long ago was interpreted to ban business pollution of waterways, was not enforced even once until 1969! You can go through the federal statutes and discover one provision after another that's never been enforced. The point is that we should first find out the extent to which laws are being complied with. Then we can decide whether they need enforcement, amendment, or repeal. This is important in evaluating the performance of our legal institutions.

Bell: I share Nader's concern, but we should clearly distinguish the important from the unimportant violations of law. It has been said you could shut down any city in the United States merely by forcing everyone to observe every letter of every law!

Nader: We can make such a separation. But let us take one priority topic—municipal corruption. Mayors and councilmen are being indicted widely for taking bribes. Who is giving those bribes? One of business's violations of law has been bribery in partnership with public officials. (It takes two to tango!) Business may fear to be "shaken down" by public officials, or it may pay for the passage—or defeat—of laws, regulations, licenses, and other favors.

Linowitz: It is very important that people in high office—in corporations or in government—set the right standard of behavior. If they violate the law, it has a downhill effect. Also, we should not construe isolated cases of business misbehavior as typical.

Jacoby: I suggest that we now go directly into the matter of priorities, without delving too deeply into particular topics: What topics need prior attention in any program to improve the business-government relationship?

Noll: One problem deserving a high priority is how to reduce the cost of representation of particular interest groups before governmental agencies charged with making social policy decisions. At present, groups with small resources lose out to groups with large resources. For example, the private line competitors to AT&T win their cases before the Federal Communications Commission and the courts; but they are being bankrupted because AT&T keeps the legal process going for years.

Blumenthal: I urge strongly that public financing of election campaigns be given attention. We all know the corrupting influence of private financing. Yet business has not spoken up to eliminate this cancer in the body politic.

Jacoby: Do you see this mainly as a problem of research, or as one of education and political action?

Blumenthal: Both. Research is required to answer many questions not yet resolved; and it should extend over the financing of state and local as well as federal election campaigns.

Bell: One reason why election campaigns are so expensive in the United States is that they are so prolonged. They should be made shorter, as in Britain.

Blumenthal: One simple but effective reform would be to make it a crime to contribute more than a few dollars in any form other than a bank check.

Weidenbaum: More imagination is needed. If Xerox buys hours of prime television time for four programs on the United Nations, why can't it buy thirty minutes each for the Democratic and Republican candidates for President and treat the expense as public service advertising?

Blumenthal: All that is required is a revision of the U.S. statutes.

Nader: Why not hold a widely publicized conference sponsored by businessmen on political "shakedowns," where it's all brought out into the open—the paying-off of building inspectors, food inspectors, customs officials, and so on? The whole system is now endemically corrupted. If one started at the top, as a kind of traumatic initiative, people would get over the inhibition against publicizing shakedowns.

I suggest that drawing boundaries between the public and private sectors, and governmental regulation by market forces instead of commissions, should be two high-priority topics. An exploration of new forms of mixed public-private enterprises is also important, including new forms of cooperatives. Much of the U.S. economy is now organized along cooperative lines, including savings and loan societies and mutual life insurance companies; but it is questionable whether their customers—depositors and policyholders—have adequate safeguards. Thus the development of a political process for electing directors to such public corporations as TVA or the New York Port Authority might improve their accountability to the people and their performance.

Ramo: I believe it important to implement the planning function in government and business. Although businessmen talk much about planning ahead, many fail to take plans seriously. It's even worse in government, where attention is focused on the crisis of the moment. Two years ago I was invited to help advise whether a new not-for-profit national center for planning should be created. Although top federal government officials supported the idea, they believed that the government should not engage in planning, because it might suggest to the world that the United States was moving toward a controlled economy. It was also decided to drop the word "planning" in favor of a center for the study of "alternatives and priorities." Although the concept was valid and important, it was not implemented. When the chips were down, not enough people had the interest to work for the establishment of the center.

Bell: I believe that ours should be a "planning" society, but not a "planned" society. The semantic distinction is between an ongoing process and a finished product.

Ramo: Our social evolution is going to get "planned" one way or another, either *for* us or *by* us. Also, while much of the future is unpredictable, there is also much that is simply unpredicted—which can be foreseen and acted on.

Fitzhugh: Three topics merit prior attention: One is how government, business, and labor unions can help to improve productivity, and thus reduce inflation. Another is public education on the roles of business and government in American society. A third is public education in the complex structure and processes of American government, which is truly the "ultimate conglomerate."

Weidenbaum: A topic deserving study is lessons for governmental control of business to be learned from the defense establishment. The most closely regulated enterprise in the United States is not Pacific Gas and Electric, but Lockheed! Government officials review and approve the details of the internal management of defense contractors. What have been the results?

Noll: We should not oversimplify. It is misleading to describe the military-industrial relationship as "regulation." The solutions needed to improve the military-industrial relation are quite different from those needed to improve public utility regulation.

Ramo: Perhaps so, but much can be learned from examining the relations of the Pentagon, NASA, and the former AEC to business. The probability that multibillion-dollar technological projects will be developed in the field of energy makes it urgent to learn all we can from the business-government relationships that have existed in other areas of technological activity. We should not assume that Lockheed is typical of all military-industrial relationships. The Department of Defense must face up to the need for reconstructing the aerospace industry.

Jacoby: It can accomplish this by adopting different procurement policies and breaking up its contracts. The "package procurement" concept under which Lockheed built the C5A transport plane was a disaster for all concerned.

Ramo: There are many issues to be studied, such as cost sharing, DOD-financed research and development that is applied to civilian products, procurement contracts with built-in motivations for productivity and efficiency, "buy-in" bidding, and so on. A recent blue-ribbon commission reported on some of these matters. This vast body of experience can teach us much about business-government relationships.

Rice: I agree with the idea of learning from experience, but I caution against applying defense-industrial relationships uncritically to energy problems. The Department of Defense has created its own demand, whereas the public creates the demand for energy. Also, there are market prices for the various sources of energy and there is competition among the sources. One can apply a market test to the success of a coal gasification project, for example, but not to the Poseidon project.

Ramo: That is true. But suppose the energy program budgets $X billions for the development of nuclear breeder reactors by, say, 1990. One cannot be sure they will be available at that time to compete with other kinds of energy. So there *is* an analogy to a weapons system.

Heyns: The trends we have been discussing have increased the number and the range of the *contacts* between government and industry. Therefore, the number of *conflicts* will increase. Our society typically responds to conflict with new legislation or with litigation; but this is an enormously expensive method of conflict resolution. (An example is the economic and social costs of Affirmative Action employment programs.) Should we not address ourselves to less costly alternative ways of resolving conflicts, such as compulsory arbitration or conciliation techniques?

Boulding: What we're talking about is evaluative studies to find which way is better. I have given up hope of optimization or maximization; all I want to know is whether we are going up or down! This is often hard to know because an adequate theory of the social system is lacking. It has to be a theory of ecological succession—which institutions and processes prosper and which do not. Economic theory is bad because it is mainly static equilibrium and not dynamics.

Economics is the only social science that has the gall to advance normative propositions. We have a highly unified social system, and the division among the various social disciplines is preposterous and arbitrary. We speak of the "environment" of business, but there is no such thing—there is only a system of interacting institutions. And when one intervenes into the system, he may readily do damage to it. Indeed, intervention often is counterproductive. I have formulated a "law of political irony"—everything you do to hurt people, helps them; and everything you do to help people, hurts them!

The other respect in which all social theory, and especially economics, is fantastically deficient pertains to distribution of the national income. For example, we do not have an agreed theory of profits that makes sense. We also lack knowledge of the distributional consequences of public policies, and of their integrational consequences—whether they add to or subtract from social cohesion. Without adequate theory, all of the empirical work in the world will be useless. And one cannot buy theory—it's the one thing that is not available on the market.

Jacoby: Your paper laid great emphasis on the dynamics of legitimation as a subject of inquiry. How would you tackle that subject?

Boulding: I really do not know how to do it. A sociologist like Bell will have ideas about that. The sociologists have been corrupted by the tendency of economists to regard all social activity as exchange. But there are many social relationships that are not exchanges.

Jacoby: A fascinating observation in your paper was that government gains legitimacy by exacting sacrifices from people. How can business exact sacrifice?

Boulding: It's a difficult problem. As Schumpeter said, the only trouble with capitalism is that nobody loves it. Or, as Birdzell put it, it has no constituents.

Birdzell: Our problem is that we are trying to understand a social relationship without a theory of the social system. We are like chemists before Lavoisier, or like biologists before Mendel. We simply do not know the genetics of organizations. We proceed empirically by trial and error, often failing and sometimes succeeding in devising viable organizations.

A useful kind of research would be to determine why profit-seeking joint stock corporations—what I call "investor cooperatives"—have evolved in all countries that have offered them freedom to evolve. Such knowledge might shed light on the role of profits and on the respective roles of business and government.

Three other issues deserve attention in an effort to improve the business-government relationship: political contributions, inflation, and taxation. The taxation and inflation problems seem to be highly interrelated in the sense that almost all obvious ways of dealing with inflation through taxation are politically objectionable because they hurt the lower-income groups in society. I offer this idea: We have made a basic mistake in basing our major federal tax on income rather than on spending. We should study the possibility of shifting the base to consumption spending, on the theory that this would foster saving and capital formation. We should regard spending on investment as something to be taxed lightly, if at all. This reform might take some poisonous slivers out of the fingers of business-government relations. Inflation is a second important cause of lack of confidence toward government and business. I am confident we can overcome it if we are willing to endure the associated hardships. [We have already discussed the third cause—political contributions.]

Jacoby: Irving Fisher defined "income" as spending, on the theory that nothing you receive counts, only what you enjoy. Nicholas Kaldor wrote a book right after World War II proposing to base British "income" taxation on consumption expenditures, in order to foster investment.

Birdzell: If J. Paul Getty wants to live on the same scale as a middle-income manager, lets tax him that way, and forget his titles to vast resources.

Boulding: You would have to reform inheritance taxes, too.

Nader: Considering that corporate income taxes have withered away as a proportion of federal tax revenues, how would business feel about abolishing this tax?

Neal: I think business would generally favor a move in that direction, but not necessarily abolition. There are good effects in a low-rate corporate income tax.

Meyer: It's been said that "the best tax is an old tax," because patterns of resource use and consumption will have readjusted to it. This is an argument against radical surgery on the federal tax system.

Nader: In general, businessmen make decisions that they believe will increase sales and minimize taxes. Tax consequences often dominate decisions. Much bad resource allocation and waste have occurred in our economy because one could "write it off." The federal corporate tax system has matrixed into a pattern of behavior that could well be done away with.

Meyer: You should not stop with the corporate tax, because your argument also applies to the personal income tax. The weight of economic opinion today favors movement to a simpler, broad-based, low-rate personal income tax. The problem is how to move from where we are to that more desirable state.

Nader: Why should we tax spending? Why not tax wealth?

Birdzell: The effect of capital investment is to increase the GNP in proportion to labor, and to increase labor's share of disposable personal income. So it is a desirable policy objective. And that's the main reason for orienting the tax system to the encouragement of investment.

Jacoby: The Europeans have moved in this direction by replacing corporate income taxes with value-added taxes. If they found that it was politically feasible to make this transition, we might also.

We must now terminate this discussion. Before we convene tomorrow, I ask each of you to consider the twenty topics listed in the agenda, to add three more of your own choice, and then to rate seven of the twenty-three topics in the order of your perception of the priority they should receive in the program of the Norton Simon Commission.

CHAPTER 7

Implementing a Program

Jacoby: Our task this morning is to outline a strategy for implementing a program to improve the U.S. business-government relationship. Let us assume that the topical content of the program has been determined. Then there are these questions: What relative weighting should be put in the program upon research to discover new knowledge, upon the synthesis of knowledge in the existing literature, and upon dialogues, conferences, and other means of educating people? Who and where are the people best qualified to staff the program? What institutions in our society could collaborate helpfully? What time dimensions should the Norton Simon Commission have in mind? What financial requirements need to be met? And how can the influence of the program be maximized?

Neal: In a CED project on technological innovation, we studied the question: What is conducive to innovation? Many case studies show one important factor is *perceived need*. Another is *adequate resources*. The scientific knowledge base ranked low, because it appeared adequate for achieving most innovations. For this reason, I would opt for a very low research component in the program. We already know so much more than we are able to use. The big problem is how to achieve change in the right direction.

Bell: I second that motion. The important thing is to pick out policy issues that are central, to develop consensus on the nature of needed reforms, and then to dramatize the matter.

Noll: I disagree with the assumption that we now know pretty much all that we need to know. We know almost nothing about how the structure and powers of a government agency relate to its performance. Take air pollution control authorities as an example. Every single air shed in the country now has one, and they are incredibly different in structure and function. We have no idea of the relation between their structures, powers, and budget levels, on the one hand, and the amount of reduction in air pollution they have achieved on the other. The same can be said about water basin authorites.

Another issue we know practically nothing about is the effects that private contributions to political campaigns actually have had upon the policies of candidates and the outcomes of elections. Until this knowledge is developed by research, we cannot know how to reform the financing of election campaigns.

Bell: Although there have been relatively few studies of air and water pollution authorities, because they are rather new, there have been many studies of political campaign contributions. Let us not set up a false issue about research. What is needed most is a statement of the major issues of principle that are involved, and a statement of the standards we seek to apply. Then we can know how to direct our research.

Weidenbaum: Much can be done to synthesize and evaluate existing knowledge, and to apply the results to public and private policy.

Rice: I would agree. There are a lot of data around that can be supplemented and pulled together to shed light on the issues. There is also need for continuing research on many phenomena we have been discussing. But synthesis and education deserve the most emphasis in the Commission's program.

Meyer: The Commission should not fall into the trap of setting a short deadline for its actions, and then acting prematurely. It is better to take the time to execute its program properly. My advice is that the Commission should first select the topics it intends to focus upon, then choose an executive director to study these topics and identify gaps in knowledge. He could then retain the best people to fill the gaps.

Ramo: In designing a program, the Commission should remember that current events in the real world will shape the business-government relationship to an important degree. Examples are detente with China, trade with the Soviet Union, and the energy problem, in which policies are as yet unsettled. The Commission could make an early impact if it focused attention on such issues.

Fitzhugh: I strongly favor a program of education and action rather than of research. We need to act on the research that has already been done.

Rice: I counsel the Commission not to institutionalize itself and turn out reports, but to perform the role of catalyzing the processes by which social reforms get made.

Bell: The nature of the Commission's program will depend heavily upon the topics selected. Some topics will be action-oriented, some legislation-oriented, and some research-oriented.

Jacoby: Ramo's comment reminds me that we haven't discussed the business-government relationship in the multinational setting.

Bell: On that subject, I will forecast that international economic problems will become so important in the next decade that business will become an instrument of national policy to an unprecedented degree. There will be worldwide problems of raw material shortages, of monetary and financial disruptions, of the use of commodity boycotts for political ends, and so on. The business-government relationship will take an entirely new turn, particularly for large corporations.

Meyer: I agree. But if the Commission makes these a subject of study, the international aspects are so complex that they would absorb all of its resources.

Bell: The emerging international order will affect the whole American business community—not merely multinational firms that do business abroad.

Heyns: I wish to make it clear that the Commission has not made any decisions, and that its program, director, emphasis, publications, and so on, all remain open for discussion.

Blumenthal: It's difficult to advise the Commission on strategy for implementing a program without knowing the budgetary and time dimensions of its work. While I would certainly select the business-government relationship in the international arena as a most important topic for study, many persons and groups are already involved with it. For that reason, I advise the Commission to confine its studies to the relationship between business and government in the United States.

Steiner: I wish to speak in behalf of dialogues and conferences as promising instruments by which the Commission could influence the course of events. They bring people with diverse points of view together. These exchanges result in some accommodations and consensus, and can lead to action.

Nader: I agree with Fitzhugh that the important thing is to get people "shook up" so they want to get things done. One preliminary step this Commission should take is to communicate with the directors of other commissions on public policy that have functioned over the last ten years, and find out why they failed to produce any action. I was close to the National Commission on Automation, sponsored by the Department of Labor in the 1960s. It had a million dollars, its people worked hard, and it published about ten volumes of material. But, historically, it has evaporated, leaving no trace.

Another proposal is that the Commission develop a theory of social change, and of the driving forces for change, and pick the topics in its program in terms of that theory.

Still another suggestion: If the Commission wishes to be a catalyst, it could offer business school students $1 thousand each for a paper on improving the business-government relationship. For $1 million you could get 1,000 papers. Business school students have so far been an inert force; they have a great potential, and some excellent ideas might be forthcoming. A Commission founded by Norton Simon should generate waves throughout society, and act as a traumatizer, just as he has done.

Finally, I suggest that the Commission would perform a valuable function by organizing available information and giving it publicity and visibility. By acting as an initiating, agitating, catalyzing, distributing agency, the Commission will get the largest results from its available resources.

Bell: I have been shaken by Nader's comment on the Commission on Automation, because I was a member of it and was a coauthor of its report. That commission's problem was to demonstrate to liberal groups that automation would *not* wipe out several million jobs; and also to show the fallacy in the argument being advanced by other liberal groups that American society was developing such abundance that nobody would need to work anymore. We put the increase in productivity in proper perspective. That commission was also the first to put forth the recommendation of public service employment, and of social indicators—subjects now being widely discussed.

Nader: I cited the Commission on Automation not because its publications lacked good ideas, but because they were very inadequately distributed and publicized. Apart from a circle of scholars and government officials, no one read them or knew about them.

Neal: As a person who has long been in the commission-on-public-policy business, I would like to suggest some steps that need to be taken, if not to insure success at least to avoid disaster. The first step the Commission should take is to choose perhaps three topics for its program. Then, find out from foundations, governments, and other sources whether a study of any one of them has already been preempted. If not, then I would study the *most successful* efforts in the field of public policy implementation, and I would seek to emulate their methods in implementing the topics in my program.

May I cite two very successful efforts of the CED that involved a heavy business-government relationship—the Employment Act of 1946 and the Marshall Plan of 1948. It was members of the CED who took leadership in the enactment of the Employment Act which, for all of its failures in execution (such as the current high rate of inflation) has improved the performance of the U.S. economy significantly.

The personal effort of important businessmen, who went against the current of business opinion and laid their reputations on the line, was crucial in this effort. The success of the Marshall Plan called for the same dedicated personal effort by leading businessmen, such as Paul Hoffman, William Foster, and David Zellerbach. In neither of these cases was the publication of a CED report a key element in the outcome. The Norton Simon Commission might well consult some of these men to obtain their experience and their advice.

Another "success story" of the CED concerned the pay of senior officials in all three branches of the federal government. Too low ceilings and too much compression in salary ranges at the upper levels were repelling the talented people needed to run our government. A formula was developed by a CED advisor and spelled out in a page-and-a-half policy statement. This served to break the logjam on congressional, judicial, and senior executive pay.

I have two caveats: First, I believe that anything less than a five-year effort would be less than optimal—five years may be too little. Second, the Commission will need a minimum of $400,000 a year to mount a significant program, and preferably more.

Linowitz: I have had the experience of serving on a dozen commissions, and I've been chairman of at least five. And I've watched commission reports gathering dust on shelves. When I joined the Norton Simon Commission, it appeared to me there were at least four subjects it could investigate: First, what is the true status of business-government relationships today? Second, how is the relationship perceived by the public? Third, what *should* the relationship be? Fourth, and the toughest question: How do we *make* the relationship what it should be?

If our Commission is going to accomplish *change,* I believe it should at the outset establish a relationship with another action-oriented organization, such as the National Association of Manufacturers, the U.S. Chamber of Commerce, the CED, the League of Women Voters, the Conference Board, Ralph Nader, or John Gardner.

We should agree on objectives and on how we can act as a catalyst. Two personal experiences lead me to this conclusion. I was a cofounder about ten years ago of the International Executive Service Corps, which sends retired American executives to foreign countries to work with local enterprises. It has been extraordinarily successful. About seven years ago I served as chairman of the National Committee for International Development, which was a private group of business leaders formed to support the U.S. foreign aid program. We advertised and we lobbied in the Congress and in the executive branch. We played a significant part in getting foreign aid bills passed.

Meyer: The question: Why did previous commissions fail? is loaded. How does one define "failure" or "success"? I served on the Population Commission, and I guess we scored a great success because—like the Automation Commission—we identified a nonproblem! We initially thought overpopulation would be a great U.S. problem; but as we proceeded in our deliberations, U.S. population growth stopped. Whether a commission succeeds or fails may be due to fortuitous events or to factors outside its control.

I feel uneasy about "traumatizing" action. Bad mistakes have been made in public policy because we acted before we knew what we were doing. There are endless examples: auto emissions, water pollution standards, housing programs, drug testing, and so on. I see this Commission's role not necessarily as one of getting immediate action, but as one of starting a dialogue.

Nader: A vitally important factor in the success of this Commission will be its ability to *communicate* effectively with the public. Commissions have often been ineffective in the past because their reports have been ponderous and have lacked specific examples and proper names which spark public interest. A very small citizen group in Boston called Action on Children's Television, working on a shoestring budget, has been highly effective in bringing about reforms because it cites real programs and actual examples. What is needed is an action philosophy, a belief that problems can be solved, instead of scholarly detachment.

Meyer: There are many ways in which policy recommendations are translated into political action, and I doubt whether one can generalize about the process.

Birdzell: Before the Commission approaches any action organization, it should identify a short list of subjects about which there is adequate knowledge and for which there is an important public interest in improving performance. Another requisite is to involve in conferences and dialogues on those subjects people who represent the interests affected and who are in a position to follow through with political action. The Commission should select subjects on which it is possible to generate a consensus, and not waste its resources fighting endless battles. I think that if the U.S. Chamber of Commerce and Nader could agree on anything that was good for the country, we could probably get it done! There are many areas where we are not "farming as well as we know how to." The Commission can contribute by building on reports that have already been written.

Jacoby: I wish to ask Birdzell what topics satisfy his two criteria of an adequate foundation of knowledge and an active public interest in reform.

Birdzell: One is an anti-inflation program; another is radical tax reform.

Boulding: Although I've enjoyed this dialogue enormously, the relationships between business and government are way down my list of priorities. If I ask myself: What are the possible sources of catastrophe during the next century? the business-government relationship is far down the line. I'm afraid this isn't very helpful to the Commission!

Bell: Well, we are all tired of apocalyptic problems we can't deal with. Maybe this is a quiet issue we can do something about.

Neal: I'll nominate one catastrophe that definitely involves the business-government relationship: What will the world be like by the year 2000 when we have transferred its major resources to the Arabs?

Ramo: I was going to remark that the business-government relationship is regarded by the public as rather a boring subject, because it affects people only indirectly. It's as though a community is ridden with an epidemic disease, and someone decides to study the doctor-hospital-population relationship there. The study may be basic to the prevention of future epidemic disease, but people want to know how to cure the disease that afflicts them *now*. It is necessary to deal with more than generalities; one must tackle actual unresolved problems.

Linowitz: I disagree that business-government relationships are a boring subject. The much-publicized Watergate episode illustrates a malfunctioning of the business-government relationship that is of intense public interest.

Birdzell: I agree that the Watergate corruption, and what Karl Popper called the "paranoid" or conspiratorial approach to society, is "center stage" today. These are by-products of a malfunctioning in the system. The way to improve both business-government relationships and the public image of them is to improve *performance* of the functions that affect the public, such as inflation or energy shortages.

Ramo: Choosing subjects of a program that one hopes will influence affairs for the better in this country *does* require attention to the audience you wish to influence.

Weidenbaum: I hope the Commission will not design its program to get maximum publicity, but will choose a program that is most important for the public welfare, and then worry about how to get publicity. In a period when our society confronts fundamental challenges, it is vital that its two most powerful institutions cooperate effectively.

Noll: I agree with Ramo that the Commission should deal with real problems. And those real problems should be ones for which the climate for reform is ripe. They must be problems on which the Commission can make an impact, and on which it takes a long-term perspective. A final requisite is that the Commission marshal the facts, and analyze them in new ways. For example, the Carnegie Commission on Educational Television was successful because its report was very specific on the nature of a public broadcasting system in the United States, its costs, and its products.

Jacoby: So far, we have had a very useful discussion of strategies that the Commission could adopt to implement its program. Perhaps we should devote the balance of our time to a discussion of topical priorities in the program. First, I shall request Professor Kovach to report her collation of your individual ratings of topics.

Kovach: There were 15 responses. The 7 subjects receiving the largest number of points were, in order, as shown at the top of p. 161. After the preceding seven topics, ratings fell off rather sharply.

Jacoby: Let us now turn to the criteria by which the Commission should select topics for its program. One criterion already suggested is importance to the public welfare. Another is public interest in the sub-

Priority	Topics	Points
1.	Reform of Governmental Regulation of Business	86
2.	Conditions of Business-Government Collaboration in Resolving Social Problems	79
3.	Public Finance of Election Campaigns	73
4.	Adoption of Growth-Oriented Taxation Policies	72
5.	Design of New Types of Public-Private Enterprises	72
6.	Implementation of the Planning Function in Government and Business	62
7.	Education for Leadership in Government and Business	52

ject. Still another is the existence of a body of basic knowledge that makes extensive research unnecessary. What are others?

Meyer: Another is the timeliness for action on the subject.

Ramo: The centrality of the business-government relationship to the topic is an obvious criterion.

Rice: The criterion of an adequate basis of existing knowledge deserves some elaboration. It is one thing to know about a real problem and its dimensions, implications, and impacts. It is quite another thing to know what to do about it. Take public financing of election campaigns as an example. I am *not* sure that we know a better way to finance them than the current system—perhaps with better policing.

Birdzell: Public financing of election campaigns is a good subject for the Commission's agenda, but it's not an easy one. The idea that millions of dollars of gifts "purchase" the donor's viewpoint by support of candidates for Congress is a fallacy. In about 99 out of 100 cases, the donors already hold the candidates' viewpoints.

Blumenthal: I demur from the preceding comments. There is no doubt in my mind that there *is* a better way of financing elections than the one used now. The fact that we do not yet know it provides all the more reason for working on the problem.

Nader: Another criterion by which the Commission should select subjects in its program is the degree to which students of the Graduate School of Management can be utilized.

Heyns: So far, eight different criteria of selection have been named. I suggest that we write them on the blackboard, and then discuss how to score the seven preferred topics in terms of those criteria.

Jacoby: While that is being done, let us discuss two topics that have so far slipped between the cracks of our dialogue. They are: relationships between multinational firms and national governments; and lessons to be learned from business-government relationships in other large market economies, such as those of Britain, France, Germany, and Japan.

Meyer: I lumped those two subjects together in my mind, and dismissed them on the ground that they are too complex and would swallow up the Commission's resources. Blumenthal also advised this.

Neal: I believe that the multiple-government relationship with large corporations deserves a middle priority.

Blumenthal: A comparative study of business-government relationships in other countries is a fascinating field of study, but I doubt that many insights useful in the United States could be derived from it. Whether one considers Japan, or France, or another nation, the business-government relationships are part of the total fabric of their societies. They reflect their own histories, philosophies, and social structures, and would not be a guide to action in the United States.

Heyns: I agree with Blumenthal. The possibility of building a French-type business-government relationship in the United States is at least two generations away. Our country lacks enough sense of community in national leadership to make the French system work here. We did not all graduate from the Ecole Polytechnique, which is what makes the French system work.

Ramo: It seems to me that multinational business-government relations rate high by many of the criteria we have established. However, I agree that a comparative study of business-government relations in foreign countries would not be fruitful, because this nation is evolving uniquely. I would like to apply Nader's idea of an essay contest to the subject: How To Finance Election Campaigns. Why shouldn't the Commission attempt to get fresh thinking in this manner?

Jacoby: I'm sure Neal will recall the Pabst essay contest after World War II, which was a precursor of the Employment Act of 1946. Pabst invited economists to submit ideas for economic institutions and policies that would improve the performance of the U.S. economy. Herbert Stein, formerly Chairman of the President's Council of Economic Advisors, won first prize. Maybe a "Norton Simon Essay Contest" would be fruitful.

Neal: Twenty years ago the CED commissioned fifty papers from scholars all over the world on the theme: What is the Most Important Economic Problem to be Faced by the United States in the Next Twenty Years? The papers were published in two volumes. We put the volumes through five printings and they were still selling madly when we took them off the market!

Steiner: Another operational idea is to commission a specialist to prepare a "position paper" on a subject of interest to the Commission. Then, a group of scholars could act as a research committee to guide his work through several drafts until it expresses a substantial consensus of the group.

Noll: A variant of that idea is to assign the same topic to a number of people. Each will write his own paper. Then they will come together and debate the merits of each paper.

Jacoby: Let us turn our attention to the matter of grading each of the seven selected topics in terms of the eight criteria of selection that have been suggested.

Ramo: If something useful is to be done on the subject of financing election campaigns, it will involve much more than business-government relations.

Blumenthal: I agree. The sources of finance are not only business firms; they include labor unions and many individual "sugar daddies." Yet I suspect that the single most corrupting influence is gifts by business.

Meyer: If you include producers' cooperatives as "business," I think you are right.

Blumenthal: One must include many others in addition to large corporations—the trade associations, cooperatives, and the labor unions. Despite the fact that the nation is still in the midst of election financing scandals, week after week requests come across my desk for contributions to luncheons and dinners to benefit men who are supposed to do something for my company.

Birdzell: The political influence of big corporations is generally exaggerated. We should remember that the real political power in the oil industry is the 10,000 or so "independent" producers—not the major oil corporations. Also, most of the millions of dollars contributed to the Committee for the Reelection of the President came from wealthy persons *without* a corporate affiliation, rather than from executives of the top 200 or 500 corporations. Perhaps Nader has studied how much came from each group.

Ramo: Also, we should recognize that business executives have their own *personal* political convictions, and it is their right to express them through campaign contributions. These should not be lumped in with "business" contributions.

Nader: That is why there is no meaningful breakdown possible between "business" and "nonbusiness" contributions. Also, how does one evaluate services to political candidates in kind, such as a loan of speech writers, airplanes, and so on?

Neal: Money is not the important campaign contribution of a labor union. A union can mobilize people to ring doorbells and get out the vote. It can influence its own membership in the normal course of its operation. Its contribution to a candidate can be huge, even if no cash payment is involved.

Noll: The central flaw in our political system is not bribing a politician to do something he thinks is wrong by giving him a big campaign contribution. It is the fact that the votes of some people are magnified.

Jacoby: I suggest that we return to criteria for selecting projects to study. One is *preemption* of a topic by other agencies in society.

Neal: The Citizens Research Foundation has been active in research on election campaign financing. And Common Cause has made this a major concern. CED has also done something on the subject.

Jacoby: What about reforming governmental regulation of business? The Brookings Institution has been active in this field.

Noll: Brookings has completed that program. It did not do nearly enough. The subject is certainly not preempted.

Rice: Much remains to be done on the effects of different structures of regulatory commissions upon the performance of regulated industries.

Noll: Most of the books published in the Brookings' series, "Studies in the Regulation of Economic Activity," are on the scholarly side, not action-oriented. They do provide an intellectual, factual basis for action by an agency that wishes to translate this work into public policy.

Fitzhugh: The subject: Education for Leadership in Government and Business, probably needs more attention than any other on the list, but one could not make much of an impact on it with $2 million spent over five years.

Nader: One way to avoid the preemption problem is to deal with new and important subjects that others have neglected. I repeat the suggestion I made yesterday: to convene a businessman's conference on business-government bribery and payoffs. Such a conference could be the trigger for a process of social reform. Newark, New Jersey, has been one of the most corrupt municipalities in the nation. Now it's coming back, because a few people said, "We've had enough. We are going to the district attorney." There are district attorneys all over the United States, ready to act once they get the facts and know that they have some citizen support.

Neal: This idea can be tested in a particular district of a large city with a sympathetic district attorney.

Jacoby: In the next few minutes, let us each cudgel his brains and *reorder* the seven high-priority topics that were selected in light of our discussion of the eight criteria of selection. Please hand your final schedule to Professor Kovach, and she will tabulate the results and report them at the luncheon which follows this session. I now return the chair to Dean Williams.

Williams: On behalf of the members of the Norton Simon Commission, I thank each of you deeply for your contribution to this very exciting intellectual exercise. Your help will be of inestimable value to us in planning and carrying out the Commission's work.

Part IV

THE PRODUCT

CHAPTER 8

The Consensus
on the Major Issues

Readers who have studied the papers submitted by participants in the UCLA Seminar on the Business-Government Relationship, and who have read the ensuing dialogue, probably are now considering how this far-ranging colloquy can be recapitulated. Summing it up is a delicate and difficult task, to be undertaken with caution. The summarizer must try to avoid errors in interpreting the views of the participants; and he must avoid interjecting his own biases. However, it is necessary to attempt a recapitulation, if the product of the seminar is to take on a distinct and recognizable character, and is not to remain a mere jumble of unconnected ideas and proposals.

We propose to recall, in turn, the major issues on the agenda of the seminar, which were set forth in Chapter 1. Then, we shall endeavor briefly to present the propositions pertaining to each issue upon which there appeared to be a substantial consensus among the participants.

THE CHARACTER OF THE PRESENT RELATIONSHIP

The initial question posed for discussion was: How should the present U.S. business-government relationship be characterized? A bewildering variety of descriptions were given. Government and business in the United States were variously described as enemies, antagonists, opponents, and adversaries. The participants used colorful analogies to describe the relationship, varying from guerrilla warfare, to the medieval church and state, to the tension between labor unions and business managements, to porcupines making love (very, very carefully!).

There was general agreement, however, that the current business-government relationship could well be described as "adversary" in nature. Officials of government characteristically look upon themselves as probers, inspectors, taxers, regulators, and punishers of business transgressions. Businessmen typically view government agencies as obstacles, constraints, delayers, and impediments to economic progress, having much power to stop and little to start. A considerable measure of mutual suspicion prevails. Each adversary lacks knowledge and understanding of the role, motivation, problems, and modes of action of the other. It was universally agreed that the current relationship is seriously defective and that it must be improved if our society is to make satisfactory progress toward its goals.

THE TREND IN THE RELATIONSHIP

A second question is whether the American business-government relationship has been worsening or improving through time. Again, there was agreement among the participants that the relationship has been deteriorating. The goals and values of our burgeoning, affluent, urbanizing, and technologizing society have become more numerous, more complex, more interrelated, and harder to reconcile. As a consequence, conflicts among various interest groups in society have multiplied, trade-off relationships have become harder to measure, social priorities have become more difficult to establish, and social consensus has become harder to achieve.

Our governmental institutions, inherited from the small, relatively poor agrarian society of our past, are not coping rapidly enough with the social problems of today. Unresolved issues about energy, the environment, urban transit, housing, poverty, drug use, and crime have piled up. Government has been tardy in weighing social values, in establishing trade-off relationships, and in making the rules needed to guide the private sector. Business has often been insensitive to changing social values, and obstructive rather than facilitative in adjusting to them. A better educated and hypercritical public holds a low level of confidence in both institutions.

WELLSPRINGS OF MALFUNCTIONING

A third basic issue is how changes in the social and technological environment have affected the U.S. business-government relationship. Four major changes in the structure and values of American society since World War II have had a profound impact: *First,* a truly national society has emerged out of local and regional societies. *Second,* what Daniel Bell has called the "communal society" has arisen, marked by relatively greater emphasis upon public goods and the internalization of external costs. *Third,* the American public holds rising expectations and now considers itself "entitled" to good jobs, excellent housing, and other amenities. *Fourth,* there has emerged a deep concern for the quality of life.

These value changes have multiplied the number of *political* decisions that have to be made relative to the number of decisions made in *markets*. More of the political decisions are unpopular because they involve clashes of conflicting interests in which *everyone* has to give up something. As a result, the political system has become clogged.

Whereas the market disperses responsibility for unpopular decisions, the political process focuses responsibility—and politicians try to evade it. Hence, we have the current crisis in the political system.

Technological changes have also played an important role. Designing new modes of urban mass transit, creating new cities, reducing environmental pollution, developing new energy supplies and controlling the new information technology—all these tasks call for innovations in governmental structures and some need public-private joint ventures. Technological changes are also forcing the need for new institutions of *international* decision making and management, especially in respect to the new satellites in the sky used for communication, navigation, weather prediction and control, and the assessment of natural resources.

Many differences between U.S. business and government can also be traced to the divergence of their underlying ethical systems. Business espouses and practices individualism, whereas government operates on a collectivist ethic. The business ethic emphasizes and rewards or punishes individual *in*equalities, whereas collectivists emphasize the equality of individuals.

Finally, the malfunctioning of the business-government relationship is due in considerable degree to public ignorance of the respective responsibilities of these two institutions in our pluralistic society. This being so, better economic and political education for citizenship must be part of the remedy.

FLAWS IN BUSINESS BEHAVIOR

What features of business performance are responsible for the flawed relationship with government? Although it was clear that members of the seminar found more fault with government than with business, they were critical of many aspects of business performance. Many censured business leaders for insensitivity to changing social values, such as the public demand for less polluting and safer automobiles that emerged during the late 1960s; and for opposing instead of cooperating with government in designing regulations to express these values. Businessmen were faulted for preoccupation with short-term results—next quarter's profit-and-loss statement—rather than with their long-term performance.

The ethical behavior of businessmen in dealing with governments also received sharp criticism, particularly efforts to "buy" political favors with campaign contributions, or with promises of lucrative jobs to civil servants in regulatory agencies. Although the officials of government and of labor unions are equally culpable, it was thought that business leaders set the standards of behavior in American society and therefore bear a special responsibility. One participant argued that it was the political *weakness* of business, which lacks a constituency, that leads to excessive lobbying in order to protect its legitimate interests.

Businessmen also received adverse comment for their ignorance of government and their lack of understanding of the problems and constraints under which government officials labor. Business was also taken to task—along with government—for raising the expectations of the public to unrealistic heights through its sales promotional efforts. With respect to one widely held belief—that big business wields inordinate political power—the participants emphatically disagreed. At least since World War II, the stream of federal government legislation and regulation has contradicted the notion that big business wields the dominant influence in American society. On the contrary, many held that its political weakness should be a source of concern.

FAULTS OF GOVERNMENT

Although business was assigned a share of the blame for a relatively unproductive relationship with government, the consensus of the seminar was that the archaic structure and processes of American government bear the major responsibility. Nearly all of the participants commented upon the much heavier load of decision making that falls upon government today, and the halting, inaccurate way in which the political system translates public preferences into operational programs. The U.S. political system was variously described as a "Tudor polity," "chaotic," "overloaded," and unresponsive to the "fields of force" of contemporary life. A "horse-and-buggy" structure of state and local governments has led to a fiasco in environmental control; and it threatens to fragment the national markets that undergird the productivity of the U.S. economy. Likewise, in the rest of the world the proliferation of national governments and a strident nationalism threaten the integrity of world markets. Everywhere, *governmental structure is contradictory to the imperatives of business efficiency.*

There was unanimity in the view that government has expanded too rapidly relative to the private sector, and that its low productivity forms an increasingly heavy drag on social progress. This low productivity may be attributed, in part, to the central motive of government, which is to provide services and jobs, whatever the cost. In part, it is due to the lack of a market test of the value of government services to the public. Several participants emphasized the need to provide *incentives* for efficient administration of public programs, as well as for innovative thinking. And steps should be taken to make the tenure of civil servants less secure, so that they will be more responsive to the citizens.

The choicest terms of excoriation of government, however, were reserved for its regulation of business. There were no dissenters from the proposition that governmental regulation of business at the present time is widely inept, wasteful, and in need of radical therapy. The joint public-private management agency type of regulation—such as the ICC, the CAB, or the FPC—generally has failed to serve either the interests of the consumers they were intended to protect or the interests of the enterprises they were supposed to control. "Functional" regulation of particular business activities, such as product safety or labor relations, is a more recent development; but many government forays into this field are still on trial. A law of entropy appears to govern regulatory agencies; when new, they perform vigorously in the public interest; as they age, they degenerate into custodians and spokesmen for their respective industries. This suggests that regulatory agencies be given a limited life, extensible only after a periodic congressional appraisal demonstrates their net value to society. The regulatory process itself suffers from endemic diseases, which were described as *Penncentralization, Lockheedization, Legalization,* and *Consultantization.* It exhibits biases in favor of represented interests and against innovations.

The recent tendency of governments to compel business firms to shoulder the costs of carrying out such social programs as environmental improvement and worker safety, in order to "economize" government expenditures, is burdening American business in international competition. It is attenuating the private enterprise system. There was also a consensus among the participants that the governmental attack on big firms in concentrated industries, exemplified by the Industrial Reorganization Bill of Senator Hart and by much antitrust litigation, was counterproductive and should be abandoned. A redirection of antitrust resources to root out restrictive practices in the economy would raise productivity, reduce inflation, and enhance business-government relationships.

REPRIVATIZING GOVERNMENTAL PROGRAMS

A fundamental issue is whether the boundary line between the public and the private sectors of the U.S. economy is properly drawn. Is government attempting to produce commodities and to perform services that could more efficiently be produced by profit-seeking enterprises? The consensus of the seminar was that U.S. governments on all levels have grown too rapidly during the last decade for the efficient management of their myriad activities. During this hectic expansion, they have intruded unwisely into some fields better cultivated by the private sector.

A "reprivatization" of such functions as the design, evaluation, and administration of health and welfare services would be desirable. Other candidates for transfer to the private sector are the insurance operations of the Veterans Administration, the uranium enrichment operations of the Federal Energy Agency, and the fire protection and waste disposal services of municipal governments. It is not even clear that the U.S. Postal Service Corporation should monopolize the mails. Participants in the seminar repeatedly stressed the unique function of government to set social priorities and to establish programs; and its inherent weakness as the manager of ongoing production operations that emanate from those programs. Here, it appears, is a fruitful field for reform.

LESSONS FROM OTHER INDUSTRIALIZED NATIONS

The question was repeatedly raised whether the American business-government relationship is as productive as those in other large nations with democratic political systems and market economies. Are there features of the relationship in such countries as Britain, France, Germany, and Japan that the United States should emulate? In particular, when American-based corporations go abroad and multinationalize their operations, are they handicapped by the fact that the U.S. government adopts an attitude of neutrality toward them, whereas the governments of most foreign countries treat their companies, in effect, as instruments of their national policy?

The consensus of the seminar was quite clear that there is little of practical value that the United States can import from the business-government relationships in other countries. The reason is that the relationship between these two institutions are imbedded in the matrix of the entire social system, of which they are only a minor part. The interactions of the public and the private sectors of the U.S. economy are much more heavily determined by what goes on in the entire social system than by the actions of either business or government per se. Nations whose social systems differ from our own will develop different business-government relationships, inappropriate for transplantation to the United States. Notwithstanding this negative response to the issue, members of the seminar were quick to recognize that the United States lacks an adequate theory or model of its social system. There is an urgent need to develop such a model in order to legitimize social institutions and processes presently lacking a theoretical foundation. This is an undertaking as difficult as it is important, however, because valid social theories are rare works of personal inspiration; they cannot be bought with money.

WHAT SHOULD THE RELATIONSHIP BE?

Just as a wide variety of adjectives were employed to describe the *present* business-government relationship, so was a broad spectrum of terms advanced to characterize the *ideal* relationship. It was said that business and government should "collaborate," "cooperate," or "act in concert." The simile of a symbiote was invoked as a model, implying a mutually beneficial coexistence of these two social institutions. "Peaceful coexistence," a phrase borrowed from the literature on Soviet-American relations, was also suggested as the proper delineation of the relationship.

Participants in the seminar were quite emphatic, however, in rejecting any idea of unity, or even of confederation or partnership. These words evoked the image of an excessively close relationship between big business and big government, which would pose a threat of dominance of other social institutions and would be inconsistent with the social pluralism that has always been an American ideal. It was generally believed that a certain amount of tension and arm's-length dealing *should* characterize the government's relationship with business, just as this should be present in its relationship to such other institutions as the labor union, the church, or the university.

Some participants held that the ideal relationship is, indeed, one of "adversaries," but that it should not be obstructive or abrasive in character. While we may reasonably expect the relationship to move from guerrilla warfare to peaceful coexistence, we would not wish it to proceed to a status of outright community. Confrontation should be replaced by cooperation; not by concert or combination.

A recurrent theme of the dialogue was the unfortunate ignorance of most businessmen about the motivations, powers, and constraints of governmental officials; and of governmental officials about the competitive imperatives and the market discipline to which the businessman is subject. The general conclusion was that the leaders of both institutions require a fuller education in the differences, as well as the similarities, of leadership roles in business and in government.

TOPICAL PRIORITIES

The seminar devoted much time to the task of identifying specific topics, within the vast range of business-government interrelationships that deserved top priority for research or education. By using the iterative type of Delphi technique, it was found that seven topics were rated highest by the group. They were, in order:

1. Reform of governmental regulation of business
2. Conditions of business-government collaboration in resolving social problems
3. Public finance of election campaigns
4. Adoption of growth-oriented taxation policies
5. Design of new types of public-private enterprise
6. Implementation of the planning function in government and business
7. Education for leadership in government and business

These seven subjects were selected from a list of twenty subjects reviewed by all participants in the seminar, plus additional subjects that various participants proposed. In view of the wide range of subjects from which the selection was made, and because there was a sharp drop in the number of votes given any topic after the first seven, it is clear that there was a pronounced consensus on the importance of these seven topics. The ratings, it should be added, reflect the consensus of the participants not only on the intrinsic importance of the topics, but also on the probable productivity of research and educational efforts by the Norton Simon Commission. They were chosen, in short, because they have the potential of producing the highest social payoffs.

It is not surprising that reform of governmental regulation of business was assigned top priority. We have seen that four participants in the seminar chose to devote their papers to this subject; and a recurrent topic of the dialogue was flaws in regulation. A rising tide of public and professional economic criticism of business regulation has appeared, and a growing literature has analyzed its effects upon the economy and the society. The Brookings Institution has published numerous reports in its Studies of the Regulation of Economic Activity; and the American Enterprise Institute for Public Policy Research has published numerous Evaluative Studies. Groups of economists at several U.S. universities, notably Massachusetts Institute of Technology, the University of Chicago, and the University of California, Los Angeles, have participated in the examination.

The great preponderence of this literature is adverse in its assessment of the effects of governmental regulation upon the vigor and growth of U.S. business enterprise and its capacity to serve the demands of the public. We need not here review the many critical studies that have been published. (An illustrative bibliography appears at the end of this chapter.) The point is that a substantial scholarly literature now exists, assessing the goals, processes, and results of efforts by the federal government to control the behavior of business enterprises in different industries, or business's performance of different functions. This provides the foundation on which to build new regulatory principles and procedures or, in some instances, to curtail or abandon regulation altogether. The consensus of the seminar was that all of the regulatory agencies need a periodic "shaking up," that some should be reoriented, and others terminated.

We shall not pause to comment on the other six high-priority topics identified by the members of the seminar. All are well-known to observers of the contemporary national scene. Like reforming the regulation of business, all have been the subject of study by many governmental or private bodies. Few will dispute the need for further investigative work to fill gaps in our knowledge about these subjects, for the development of public policies with respect to them, and for education of the public in the nature of these policies.

A STRATEGY FOR CHANGE

We come, finally, to consider how a program, or series of programs, intended to improve the U.S. business-government relationship, can be implemented. What relative emphasis should be put on research to discover new knowledge, synthesis of existing knowledge, and education to communicate knowledge to those who need it? What are the desirable time dimensions and financial requirements of an effective program? What individual and institutional expertise should be called upon to make inputs? How can the influence of a program be maximized?

Although there were one or two dissentient voices, most of the conferees advised that emphasis in any program mounted by the Norton Simon Commission should be placed upon efforts to *synthesize* existing knowledge and to *communicate* it to the political and economic leaders of our society as well as to the public. American society is like the farmer who declined to take advice on better farming techniques from the county agricultural agent on the grounds that he was "not farming as well as he already knew how to!" Our universities and other institutions for public policy analysis have already developed many of the concepts needed to improve the performance of both government and business and the relationship between them.

The central need is not research to produce more knowledge, but integration of what is known and communication of the product to those able to act. As one participant said: "The important thing is to pick issues that are central, develop consensus on needed reforms, and then dramatize the matter." It was felt that the Commission should be a catalyst for action, organizing existing knowledge and giving it visibility. The Commission was advised to review the records of past commissions on public policy, in order to identify factors that led to their success or failure. Ineffective *communication* of reports to the public seems to have been a prolific cause of failure. One successful prototype was the Committee for Economic Development, which took leadership in the enactment of the Employment Act of 1946 and the Marshall Plan of 1948.

With respect to the magnitude of an effective program to improve the U.S. business-government relationship, it was believed that anything less than a five-year effort would be less than optimal, and that a minimum budget of $400,000 to $500,000 per year would be necessary.

The participants suggested that the Commission sponsor a variety of specific programs. Among some of the more striking proposals was a conference on "corporate crime," a conference on corruption in public office, and an essay contest among college students on ways to improve public-private sector cooperation. The Commission was counselled to place on its agenda only issues of immediate practical interest to large numbers of people, and to offer specific proposals to cope with these issues.

POETIC MEDITATIONS

An altogether delightful development was the submission of some poetic meditations by Professor Kenneth E. Boulding, inspired by his attendance at the seminar. As his readers well know, Professor Boulding is a master of the rhymed couplet and serves as the unofficial poet laureate of the American Economic Association. His lyrics affirm, in a poetic vein, points previously made in ponderous prose!

> The public fist is thinly gloved:
> Business, feeling much unloved,
> Thinks Government is out to get it
> And if it does we may regret it.
>
> Business, more than in the past,
> Feels itself to be harassed.
> For power to stop becomes an art
> More powerful than the power to start.
>
> When things become a little sour
> We call on countervailing power.
> And, as the tension slowly mounts,
> The countervailing is what counts.
>
> Business meets a messy fate
> If it tries to be a State;
> Business leaves us in the lurch
> When it tries to be a Church;
> Business makes itself a fool
> When it tries to be a School;
> Business drowns in love of pelf
> When it tries to be itself;
> Business might as well enjoy
> Living as a whipping boy.
>
> The imminent approach of death
> Will clear the mind and sweeten breath.
> So agencies are most effective
> That die on reaching their objective.
>
> Creating crises may be how
> We all could learn from Chairman Mao.
> So troubles should not much dismay us
> Who seek the best amount of chaos!

ILLUSTRATIVE BIBLIOGRAPHY

We cite here some pertinent recent studies of federal regulation of U.S. business:

1. Brown, Keith C. *Regulation of the Natural Gas Industry.* Baltimore: Johns Hopkins University Press, November 1971.
2. Capron, William M., ed. *Technological Change in Regulated Industries.* Washington, D.C.: The Brookings Institution, 1971.
3. Conant, Michael. *Railroad Mergers and Abandonments.* Berkeley and Los Angeles: University of California Press, 1964.
4. Friedlaender, Ann F. *The Dilemma of Freight Transport Regulation.* Washington, D.C.: The Brookings Institution, 1969.
5. Helms, Robert B. *Natural Gas Regulation: An Evaluation of FPC Price Controls.* Washington, D.C.: American Enterprise Institute for Public Policy Research, 1974.
6. Jacoby, Neil H. "Antitrust or Pro-Competition: A Positive Policy for Competition in the U.S. Economy." *Antitrust and Shifting National Controls Policies.* New York: The Conference Board, March 1974.
7. MacAvoy, Paul W., *The Effectiveness of the Federal Power Commission,* Reprint Series. Washington, D.C.: The Brookings Institution, 1971.
8. McKie, James W. *The Ends and Means of Regulation,* General Series Reprint. Washington, D.C.: The Brookings Institution, 1974.
9. Moore, Thomas Gale. *Freight Transportation Regulation.* Washington, D.C.: American Enterprise Institute for Public Policy Research (November 1972).
10. Noll, Roger G. *Government and the Sports Business.* Washington, D.C.: The Brookings Institution, 1974.
11. Noll, Roger G. *Reforming Regulation.* Washington, D.C.: The Brookings Institution, 1971.
12. Noll, Roger G., Merton J. Peck, and John J. McGowan. *Economic Aspects of Television Regulation.* Studies in the Regulation of Economic Activity. Washington. D.C.: The Brookings Institution, 1973.
13. Peltzman, Sam. *Regulation of Pharmaceutical Innovation.* Washington, D.C.: American Enterprise Institute for Public Policy Research, June 1974.
14. Peltzman, Sam. *The Effects of Automobile Safety Regulation* (Ms. August 1974).
15. Posner, Richard A. *Regulation of Advertising by the FTC.* Washington, D.C.: American Enterprise Institute for Public Policy Research (November 1973).
16. Phillips, Almarin, ed. *Promoting Competition in Regulated Markets.* Studies in the Regulation of Economic Activity. Washington, D.C.: The Brookings Institution, 1975.

Index